F 10/84   8.95

75p

Cel

On and Off the Rails

Photo: Chris Smith

On and Off the Rails

The best of
BROUGH SCOTT

London
Victor Gollancz Ltd
1984

By the same author:

THE WORLD OF FLAT RACING
(with Gerry Cranham)

ACKNOWLEDGEMENTS
All these pieces originally appeared in *The Sunday
Times* to whom grateful thanks are extended for
permission to use them here.

On and off the Rails first published in
Great Britain 1984
by Victor Gollancz Ltd,
14 Henrietta Street, London WC2E 8QJ

This selection and original material © 1984
Brough Scott

British Library Cataloguing in Publication Data
Scott, Brough
   On and off the rails.
   1. Horse-racing
   I. title
   798.4   SF334
   ISBN 0-575-03334-7

Designed by John Grain
Photoset by Rowland Phototypesetting Ltd,
Bury St Edmunds, Suffolk
Printed in Great Britain by
Billing & Son Limited, Worcester

Contents

List of Photographs

Foreword

His is the best company at the races. The races on television, that is. No one in their right minds would actually want to be with him, up hatless on some unsteady perch, battered by the winter winds of Ayr or broiled in his morning suit above the Derby crowds at Epsom. It is his words that matter, wise and experienced words, coming engagingly from so young a man (well, he looks young, dammit) who actually knows all those deadpan trainers and shifty jockeys that wouldn't willingly give the time of day to the rest of us punters.

He had a way with horses himself, going with the best of them in the sleet at Cheltenham or the murk at Newbury in the days when such giants as S. Mellor and T. Biddlecombe bestrode the paddocks. I first felt a lurch towards affection for B. Scott when he took something unexpected past the post (it may have been at Doncaster: it was foggy enough all right) and me to the unaccustomed attentions of the old £5 paying-out window. You tend to watch a promising young fellow's career after that.

And then he happened to be literate: and not only literate but polished, skilful, entertaining, turning the paragraphs out with the zest and the sheen you expect to see among the top three-year-olds in the parade ring. Now Sunday mornings are nothing without him. The hangover is unlifted, the slippered progress morose, the bed not worth breakfasting in unless there is a despatch from B. Scott to put one in touch with what it all means and why it matters.

I have no doubt that many of those reading the B. Scott output will be people who do not go racing regularly but simply enjoy and value what he says because of the way he says it. It is a gift given to very few. There were those once who took up golf only because Bernard Darwin wrote so elegantly about it. There were those who went to Roses matches only because the blessed Cardus breathed endearing life into them. There were many who watched the last round of the Open on television only because the incomparable Henry Longhurst transformed it into immediate history.

Now, on sporting occasions and Sunday mornings alike, we have their natural successor, a boon to his employers and a blessing to the rest of us—as these splendid pages now remind us.

Alastair Burnet

Introduction

How unlucky was March 13th, 1971? A cold and gloomy Saturday at Warwick, a big black brute called Bonnie Highlander in front, just two fences between us and my 101st winner as a jockey. But I had him too fast and flat at the second last. The ground came up to bite us. The game, for me, was finally over. The work that would lead to this book would have to begin.

It might have worn a nasty disguise for a week or two, but that crash was a blessing all right. Lying in an ambulance with the wooden bar between the teeth and with the knowledge that the falls were clearly out-distancing the winners, the decision was obvious. If the feeling came back into the legs and we got out of this hole, the business would have to be done on the safer side of the rails.

Looking back now at the coincidences and kindnesses that have helped me since, realising the background I had been given by eight marvellous, unexpected and not always unsuccessful years as a jockey, and remembering that poor Tom Beckett was brought to the same Warwick casualty ward three races later with injuries which proved fatal, it's absolutely no understatement to say that both before, on, and after that 13th of March, I was the luckiest fellow imaginable.

Lucky to have started on ITV with nothing more to offer than the dubious "if you can't be good, be different". Lucky to get employment on *The Evening Standard* which culminated in the fascinating, if occasionally "blood out of a stone" task of ghosting the Lester Piggott column. And doubly lucky to land the *Sunday Times* job which meant the supervision of such firm but sympathetic men as John Lovesey and now David Robson. Lovesey's gentle "I don't think you have done yourself justice" ("it's rubbish, re-write or we don't print") still haunts the memory.

But above all else I was lucky to have ever got involved in the absurd, glorious, shimmering kaleidoscope that is the racing world. Maybe it was bound to happen ever since that first Raymond Glendenning commentary, and my Dad's curses, as Galcador got up to pip Prince Simon in the 1950 Derby. Certainly it was inevitable once I had inhaled the addictive smoke that lingers when you have ridden your first winner over fences. For more than any other sport, racing is a world of its own. If you have it as your parish, you follow the chief participants literally from the cradle (or even the gleam in the breeder's eye) to the grave. Narrow it may be, but you meet mega-rich and miserable poor, triumph and disaster, jokers and villains, hope and despair. In a funny, sometimes rather grotesque, way you can hold a mirror up to life itself.

Which is why, apart from the simple flattery of the printed scrapbook, it has been such a pleasure to arrange and introduce this selection from my last ten years on *The Sunday Times* beat. Thrill for me perhaps; agony at times for Victoria Petrie-Hay and then Joanna Goldsworthy from Gollancz as they had to wrestle with my vagueness and unpunctuality. Only they can know the achievement in this book appearing at all.

George Ennor has done his usual mastermind midnight job with the corrections. Chris Smith and Gerry Cranham have produced the photographs which always matched their support on our assorted assignments. And that noted racing man, Sir Alastair Burnet, has graced the opus with a typically generous introduction.

For all of them the only hope of thanks is that these pages can give a fraction of the fun, fury, wonder and whimsy that the writer took at the time. If that also happens to any of you who read on, then the whole enterprise will have been easily worthwhile.

Brough Scott
June 1984

*At its worst, racing can seem like a minute of action
followed by an age of talk. But when it gets it right, there
really is something to talk about. Here are a few instances
when the play was worth the programme. Starting—where
else—at the greatest theatre of all, the Grand National at
Aintree. This appeared on April Fool's Day, 1973. But
there was no joke in the title.*

Red Rum . . . at the Last Gasp
April 1st 1973

As he staggered, hocks buckling, into the second enclosure, they gave him as
great a cheer as they had done his conqueror in the large winner's circle next
door. For Crisp, the giant ten-year-old black Australian gelding, had taken this
Grand National by the throat and, in his glorious and tragic defeat, had given as
much to the nerve-stretching spectacle as the bay gelding beside him who had so
determinedly attacked and finally conquered.

Red Rum's victory should not ever be decried: even though he was receiving
23lbs from Crisp. The horse, whose first visit to Aintree was when winning a
two-year-old selling race on the Flat six years ago, jumped quite perfectly and
took no less than twenty seconds off Golden Miller's 39-year-old record.

No credit can be too high for 42-year-old Donald (Ginger) McCain, who has
had a small stable at Southport for five years, has turned out a mere fifteen
winners so far, and whose main gallops are the local sands. Yet he bought Red
Rum only last August, won five consecutive races with him, rested him and, with
one preparatory race, produced him in quite superb condition yesterday. In
winning he realised, too, the life's ambition of his 85-year-old neighbour, Mr
Noel Le Mare, who besides running Glenkiln in the National, had had numerous
and costly attempts to land the Blue Riband.

Twenty-five-year-old Brian Fletcher had already won a National five years ago
on Red Alligator, but if he wins five more he could never ride a better race. His
determination ensured that he was near enough to be able to grab his chance
when the inevitable happened and the brilliance of Crisp had finally ebbed away.

I say inevitable because the tragedy and also the glory of the race was in the
problem that confronted Richard Pitman on Crisp's back. The horse is a bold and
forceful jumper who likes to bowl along with the leaders, but more significant
than this, he is used to running in the highest class over exactly half the distance of
the Grand National, so if he were to get to the front early there was no way the
horse could tell he had two laps rather than one to complete. Yet with such a
jumper it is too risky to start slowly at the back of the field and chance having very
little room to jump the first and most difficult line of fences.

So the absolutely crucial moment in this race was at the third fence, the huge
open ditch. Pitman had to allow Crisp full liberty to jump this and already he was

*Overleaf: The start of
the 1977 Derby. The
winner, The Minstrel,
is fourth from the left
(Chris Smith)*

almost in front. All 38 had set off in perfect going headed by Grey Sombrero on the opposite side to Crisp. But none of them could match Crisp's brilliant two mile speed once he had taken command and how marvellous it looked, the great black Australian flying over fence after fence and drawing farther and farther away from his field. But it was also tragic because up on the jockeys' stand I could hear the injured Tommy Stack muttering: "Jesus, there's no way he can keep up that pace for so long."

After the second Valentine it was clear that Red Rum was the only horse with any possible chance of catching Crisp. After the last, as Pitman gathered Crisp to go right-handed up the run-in, the big horse wavered with the fatal drunkenness of exhaustion. The gap was still some twenty lengths and, although Pitman did everything he knew, the big horse was now past helping. Red Rum and Brian Fletcher were attacking all the time and, as the whole of Aintree opened its lungs, they swept past and snatched the prize.

Red Rum winning the 1973 Grand National (Sport and General)

For Red Rum, of course, this was only the start. A later piece will tell how two more wins and two seconds were to make him the most famous Grand National horse of all time. For Crisp, the horse who gave Red Rum 23lbs, there was to be no Aintree return but there was one sweet day of revenge. At Doncaster that autumn he and Red Rum met again at level weights and the big Australian cruised home by ten lengths. Unfortunately Crisp also broke down in the process, so future galloping was confined to the hunting field from which he only finally departed early in 1984. That Grand National is still a marvellous, dramatic, moving memory. Flat racing doesn't often hit you like that. But here's a day that certainly did . . . Ascot, July 26th 1975, Grundy and Bustino laying it on the line.

'Come on my son!'—and Grundy does just that
July 27th 1975

Grundy's half-length defeat of Bustino in the King George VI and Queen Elizabeth Diamond Stakes at Ascot was much more than a seal to his greatness. It was the hardest, most implacable, most moving flat race that I have ever seen.

Grundy beating Bustino in the 1975 King George VI and Queen Elizabeth Diamond Stakes (Gerry Cranham)

Bustino's tactics were predictable, but his courage and strength were almost unfathomable. Led by his two pacemakers, first Highest and then Kinglet, Bustino was never further back than fourth and went to the front four furlongs out. The pace was so strong that the field was stretched at this stage and Grundy had already been pushed up close to last year's St Leger winner and Lester Piggott, on Dahlia, was also moving through to be a danger. Sweeping into the straight, Bustino and Joe Mercer set for home with a furious determination, and very soon it was obvious that only Grundy, still two lengths adrift, could prevent them taking the £81,910 first prize.

Going to the two furlong post it was also obvious that this was to be no twinkle toed, flaxen-tailed acceleration that would take Grundy past the outstretched leader, but only grit, power and sheer slogging guts.

Behind them Dahlia was running her best race of the season, but the only question that mattered to the huge crowd was whether the Derby winner could close and beat his year older opponent. With the whips out, they came to the final furlong just about level, and from high in the stand one had the feel that the older horse's slogging stamina might be too much. But then well inside the final furlong it was Bustino who began to weaken, rolling as tired horses do away from the fence and actually, for a moment, touching Grundy. It wasn't much, but it was the chink in the armour and, with Pat Eddery pressing Grundy like a man possessed, the bonny chestnut battled home to the line amid a crescendo of sound topped, of course, by trainer Peter Walwyn's frantically bellowed, "Come on my son."

Dahlia ran on to be five lengths away third, with the two other French challengers, On My Way and Card King, fourth and fifth. All these covered themselves in glory, but they were only supporting cast compared to the two stars. The mile and a half was covered in a quite astonishing time. Grundy finally clocked 2 min 26.98 sec, which is no less than 2.46 sec within the course record and 3.45 sec faster than Dahlia's 2 min 30.43 sec, which is the fastest, electrically-recorded time for this race.

Grundy's winnings now pass Mill Reef's previous record total of £312,122. Coming down in the lift to the unsaddling enclosure, trainer Walwyn mopped his brow and said simply, "They can't take it away from him now." As he loped past the crush of well wishers, he understandably didn't want to be drawn on future plans. "Who cares about the future after that?" he said. Grundy's Milanese owner, Dr Carlo Vittadini, looked similarly blissful and merely said that he favoured his colt bowing out in the Champion Stakes in October. Dr Vittadini added: "This was a bigger thrill than when Grundy won the Epsom Derby or the Irish Derby. He was meeting the best horses in Europe and did it splendidly. There has been common talk that my colt had not beaten much in the classics, but he's proved that wrong today."

Among the crush in the unsaddling enclosure, no pair looked more pleased than Sir Desmond Plummer, chairman of the Levy Board, and Douglas Gray, retiring director of the National Stud, who, of course, were party to Grundy's purchase by the National Stud at a value of only £1m. The word "only" is used advisedly as Grundy would now be conservatively assessed at £2½m.

Walwyn and Eddery pocketed their exotic trophies from the De Beers Corporation, who put up £44,000 towards this race, and continued their incredible form by winning the next race with Inchmarlo. This completed the most unbelievable fairy story of a day for Walwyn, for he had also taken the first race with Hard Day, ridden by no less a "cavaliere" than Dr Vittadini's lovely daughter, Franca.

As the horses were led away after the big race to be washed down, the buzz was as much of wonderment as of congratulation. Wonder at the way Grundy's record-breaking speed was so flawlessly complemented by his own and his rider's determination. And, perhaps, almost equally, at the magnificence of Bustino in defeat.

When Joe Mercer humped his saddle and weight cloth towards the scales, he said to me, "It was fantastic. It is the greatest race he has ever run." Like his two pacemakers, Bustino is owned by Lady Beaverbrook, whose racing manager, Sir Gordon Richards, was rapt in admiration for the big, classically-made bay colt.

"It was as good a race as I have ever seen," he said. "I wouldn't make any excuses because Grundy is a great horse, but our fellow had to go on half a mile out and, if we had only had something else to tow him just that little bit further, it might have been even closer. But he has broken the track record at Epsom and now they have broken it here, so everyone can see he is a great horse. He will just have one more race, and then the Arc de Triomphe."

After that Bustino will retire to the Royal stud at the same time as Grundy takes up his new duties at Newmarket. They are both the most tremendous assets for British bloodstock, bred as they are completely without the often considered essential trans-Atlantic influence.

British racing has many problems, but the riding and the courage and the ability shown by the two heroes in yesterday's race will be something that it can be proud of forever.

Looking back now it seems hardly surprising that such a race took its toll. Bustino never ran again and although Grundy did reappear at York he was stones below form and so also retired to stud. Ironically Bustino was the more successful in the fatherhood stakes. He remained a much sought-after consort at the Royal Stud while Grundy, despite siring an Oaks winner in Bireme, fell out of favour at the National Stud and was eventually sold to Japan in 1983.
Now to someone who did come back—Red Rum, the most popular horse of our time. He had won the Grand National

again in 1974 and was second to L'Escargot in 1975 and to
Rag Trade in 1976. Here's his final throw.

Red Rum III
April 2nd 1977

Red Rum has done it and done it clear. Yesterday at Aintree he galloped clean away with his record third Grand National amidst cheers that should live centuries longer than any of us lucky enough to be there.

At the line he and Tommy Stack had no less than 25 lengths to spare over Churchtown Boy with Eyecatcher five lengths back in the same place as last year. But long before the winning post Red Rum had shown again that he is the ultimate Grand National horse and the famous Aintree fences had reminded us that only the few survive.

In fact, although Hidden Value and Saucy Belle were remounted to finish tenth and eleventh, only nine of the 42 starters completed the course without mishap. Of the jockeys only that gallant solicitor John Carden was taken to hospital and happily no harm befell Charlotte Brew who trundled round on her pioneering female mission miles behind before she and old Barony Fort finally ground to a halt four fences from home. "We didn't finish but it was quite marvellous to have taken part," said Charlotte.

By the time the field had reached the Canal Turn, the eighth fence, it was already all too obvious that everyone was taking part in the Grand National. Fifteen horses, including the Gold Cup winner Davy Lad and our selection Sebastian V, were already out of the race and the remainder were led by the complete outsider Boom Docker and an uneasy pair of loose horses.

Strong winds and sunshine produced the quick going which Red Rum loves but also the fast pace that can be a Grand National peril. On the floor after the first were High Ken, Duffle Coat, Spittin Image, War Bonnet, the only grey Willy What and Pengrail on whom Ron Atkins had an all too brief substitution for the injured John Francome. The ditch two fences later claimed Harban, Inycarra, Royal Thrust, Burrator and Ireland's darling Davy Lad. At this stage our selection Sebastian V was in front but he was too bold at Becher's where Winter Rain and Castleruddery were also fallers. So, Boom Docker and little short legged John Williams sailed back towards the stands well ahead of the loose horses and the rest of the pack, behind whom Charlotte Brew could already be seen struggling to make her old hunter thunder along within a fence or two of the leaders. Boom Docker skipped over The Chair fence in front of the stands but Sage Merlin in second place was not so lucky, and rolled over on landing and for an awful moment seemed to be right in Red Rum's path.

The old maestro sidestepped like Phil Bennett and already we were beginning to dream of the impossible as he followed Boom Docker over the water jump close up in the following group. This team order soon took a radical reshape when the leader decided that one circuit was enough and downed tools at the first fence second time around, putting The Songwriter out of the race and leaving Andy Pandy out almost as far clear as Boom Docker had been before.

This blissful state of affairs for those who had made Fred Rimell's horse a 15–2 favourite lasted for four more fences but then Becher's once again justified its reputation, taking out first the leader, then Nereo (who was going well), Brown Admiral and Sandwilan. Who else to take the lead now but Red Rum himself? But immediately a hideous repetition of the Foinavon fiasco loomed up as he was hampered by the loose horses at the 23rd.

He was too wily for that and even though pestered by another loose horse at the Canal Turn he gave Tommy Stack a corner of which James Hunt would have been proud, and suddenly with six fences only left to jump, Red Rum was in charge and a great cry went up as everyone scanned back for dangers.

For a dizzy quarter mile he seemed to be going better than his few pursuers. But then as they came to the third last it was obvious that Churchtown Boy, who had won the Topham Trophy over the same fences only on Thursday, was going with deadly ease. His rider Martin Blackshaw told me afterwards: "I was really motoring at the time but then I never really jumped the last three." Up in front Tommy Stack had looked round once, but when he heard the crash of Church-town Boy hitting the second last he was certain that his only dangers were the loose horses or some terrible repeat of the Devon Loch disaster on the run-in.

From the stands it didn't look so easy and it was almost too hard to bear as Red Rum safely jumped the last and stormed up the run-in to his place back between the police horses and forever into steeplechasing history.

It was only afterwards that Tommy Stack's complete professionalism began to break. He had us all close to tears as he paid tribute to this incredible four-legged hero. "You know," he said, "he really loves it out there; he looks at each fence jumps it, and then looks for the next. On another course he doesn't really bother but here he knows that he is the king."

For Ginger McCain, to whom so many people have been free with their "retire Red Rum" advice, we can't give anything more than complete praise and gratitude for turning out the winner in such marvellous condition.

As an overjoyed McCain ran out to greet Red Rum he gripped me breathlessly by the arm and just muttered those three words which were echoed fifteen minutes later when the broad blue tattooed arms of head lad Taffy Williams were scraping the sweat from Red Rum's gleaming but not heaving flanks. Those words were said with a sigh and a wondering shake of the head. They were, quite simply, "What a horse!"

That was to be Red Rum's last National and he went on into magnificent old age as something of a professional celebrity, doing everything from This is Your Life *to*

*switching on the lights at Blackpool. But if 1977 saw Red
Rum still as King of Aintree, at Epsom in high summer we
had a truly royal occasion—and with almost jump-racing
excitement.*

Drama at the Jubilee
June 5th 1977

There was total drama in yesterday's Oaks with the hot favourite, Durtal, nearly
killing herself and Lester Piggott before the race, and then the Queen's Dunfermline responding to the Jubilee roar to bring a royal victory in the last few
strides.

The trouble began during the parade when Durtal was very keyed up. As
Lester Piggott began to canter her down towards the start it became obvious that
he was on something similar to a runaway train. Coming past the paddock he
tried to steady her by putting her close to the rails but in his efforts at restraint the
saddle began to slip. It finally went right under the filly and Lester with it, caught
by a foot in a stirrup iron. A second later Durtal collided with one of the big
aluminium rails and in the ensuing mêlée Piggott's foot came free. Durtal
suffered severe lacerations to her hind leg and was taken away for treatment, as
was Piggott, who walked ashen-faced from the ambulance muttering, "I'm lucky
to be alive." But there is plenty of iron beneath that leathery skin and after
missing one race he was back in the saddle again and, with a typically cheeky
finish, won the 4.25 race on Elland Road.

*Willie Carson
grinning and winning
as Dunfermline takes
the 1977 Oaks for the
Queen (Gerry
Cranham)*

The Oaks itself was won with similar resolution by Willie Carson who brought Her Majesty's home-bred Dunfermline from a seemingly hopeless position. The early running had been made by the big, awkward-striding Vaguely Deb, who managed the undulating Epsom track far better than her action would suggest. Epsom's undulations caused some bumping and Willie reported that he was twice badly hampered on Dunfermline. So, as the runners swung through Tattenham Corner into the straight, he was still many lengths adrift and Vaguely Deb kept thundering along in front chased by the French filly, Fabuleux Jane and her own stable companion, Freeze the Secret. Freeze the Secret still looked sure to win inside the final furlong but Carson and Dunfermline drew inspiration from the roar of the crowd and settled the race by three-quarters of a length on the line. Vaguely Deb was three lengths away third.

Dunfermline's success was a supremely happy one for Her Majesty for more than just Jubilee reasons. She bred this tough bay filly by Royal Palace out of her own mare, Strathcona; and the Queen bought Strathcona's dam, Stroma, on her own judgment, at Doncaster Sales. It was the first time the Queen has won the Oaks with a filly she has bred herself. The previous Oaks victory in her colours, that of Carrozza exactly twenty years ago, was from a filly leased from the National Stud. By an ironic twist, Carrozza's jockey that day was Lester Piggott. And, by an even more bitter quirk of fate, Durtal's trainer, Barry Hills, was having his second taste of Oaks disaster, for only three years ago his runner, Dibidale, looked sure to win until her saddle went round in the straight. Dibidale's rider that day was Willie Carson.

Although not so many of us have hats to throw in the air nowadays, a royal victory is still a wonderfully popular occasion. It is not always so with the big battalions and too much exposure to the high-flyers would almost make a Militant out of Debrett. But the 1978 St Leger didn't lack for cheers. Trainer Clive Brittain had won his first classic, and owner Marcos Lemos had at last got some reward for all the support he had given in those days before the Arabs came to the rescue.

Faith tears up the Form Book
September 1978

Faith can move mountains, so it doesn't have much trouble tearing up form books, and that was what happened when Julio Mariner ran home in a fast run St Leger at Doncaster yesterday. Julio Mariner's connections have always maintained that he was a horse in the classic class of his Oaks winning sister, Juliette Marny, but except for a good run first time out behind Shirley Heights and a bloodless victory in a maiden race at York, Julio Mariner has done nothing but disappoint this season, and last time out was a poor eighth of nine in the Benson and Hedges Gold Cup.

Yet here he was knifing through the field with all the flair that trainer Clive Brittain and owner Marcos Lemos have always insisted he had. He took up the running from the freshly blinkered Obraztsovy at the furlong pole, and held Le Moss by 1½ lengths at the line. Obraztsovy's stable companion M-Lolshan just pipped him for third place, the Grand Prix de Paris winner Galiani was fifth and the odds on favourite Ile de Bourbon a lifeless sixth after having every chance.

The start was held up for nearly twenty minutes after a horrific accident to the French challenger, Easter King. After rearing several times in the stalls he came clean over backwards and then lay thrashing on the ground with one of the stall handlers sitting on his head. Easter King had apparently injured his skull and with two race course vets and owner Sir Charles Clore's own vet, Mr Spike Kirby, a tranquilliser was apparently soon administered. Unfortunately, this did not appear to have much effect for some time and the wretched beast continued to thrash around with his legs, making the job of dragging him out of the way of the start extremely difficult. His rider, Phillipe Paquet, was unhurt but the other jockeys were dismounted while Easter King was dragged to the side. Finally, all the other runners were loaded up and dispatched on their fourteen-furlong journey with the luckless Easter King still thrashing around only yards away. Afterwards the tranquilliser took better effect and the horse was carted off to the stables with a suspected fractured skull and may well have to be put down.

Harsh words were exchanged afterwards for the failure to remove Easter King beforehand, either dead or alive. But since all his connections were down there, there could be no question of shooting the horse immediately without their permission and they were reluctant to give this since it was still possible that the horse was merely concussed. Others said that the horse could have been hidden from the eyes of the crowd in his agony which is a more sensible point but it is still not easy to drag a horse in a desperate trouble out of the way.

Once the race was under way the gallop was a fast one cut out by Arapahos and Lotta Continua, who was the pacemaker for Le Moss. Although Arapahos lasted longer than Lotta Continua, it was Obraztsovy who shot ahead turning into the straight immediately followed by Le Moss, who ran a predictably determined race quite unworried by the betting weakness which had seen his price drift out from 5–1 to 8–1.

At this point Ile de Bourbon was perfectly placed in fourth place and Julio Mariner only had one behind him. But it soon became clear that Ile de Bourbon's midsummer brilliance had deserted him as he struggled to make ground on the leaders. Once it became clear that he was not going to win, the question became whether Le Moss could wear down Obraztsovy but even that problem evaporated when the famous blue and white colours of Capt Marcos Lemos could be seen sweeping through the pack with victory written all over them.

Afterwards, Ile de Bourbon's jockey John Reid said, "I have no excuses. I would not have won at any distance. He was just never going." On the other hand the victorious Eddie Hide gave his famous wide tooth grin and said simply, "At last he has done everything right. You can't often go on making excuses for a horse but in his case you can. In the Derby the course and the ground were against him. At Ascot we came too soon and at York last time he wasn't himself with the blinkers on."

It was a particularly happy result for his owner Marcos Lemos, a London-based Greek shipping magnate, for he has always put tremendous faith both in English racing in general and Julio Mariner in particular. It was his first classic success and it is no flattery to say that it could not have been better deserved.

Julio Mariner retired to the rigours of stud life and Brittain and Lemos had to wait until 1984 before tasting classic success again—with Pebbles in the One Thousand Guineas.
But now a taste altogether stronger. Bob Champion's Grand National, the most extraordinary race-report I will ever have to write. Well, to be honest, it wasn't even written. In the turmoil and tears and shouting of the Aintree winner's enclosure there was no time to pen neatly spaced paragraphs. We just had to scratch a few notes on the race card and then hare off to a crackling telephone line and ad-lib away at a long-suffering typist. This is how it came out.

Champion's Battle
April 5th 1981

In what must be the most inspiring Grand National result of all, Bob Champion came back from the cancer ward, Aldaniti returned from the cripples' stall, and together they held off by four lengths the challenge of the favourite Spartan Missile and his 54-year-old owner-trainer-breeder-rider John Thorne.

Eighteen months ago I drove home from seeing the thirty-year-old Bob in his Surrey hospital and cried miserably in the car. No amount of gallant "I'll be back next year" talk could hide the feeling that in his balding emaciated state the only ride he was going to take was in a long black car. Yesterday the tears were running again, more tears than even Red Rum brought to the Grand National winner's circle, and they were tears of the purest joy.

No one could exaggerate the mountain Champion had to climb and no jockey could ever have ridden a better race, or indeed a stronger one than he did yesterday. Aldaniti is a big heavy horse and there were doubts even among his supporters that his impetuosity would be too much for him, particularly over the early fences.

Indeed, at the very first, pulling hard, he clouted the fence and pitched dangerously on landing. For watching friends it was not a promising start and yet as Bob said later, "It turned out the very best thing. It made him think and even though he was going quite free he was having a look at them and after that he really jumped super."

So well was Aldaniti going that he joined the early leader Carrow Boy and Zongalero at the Canal Turn and actually pulled his way to the front as the great cavalry charge swept towards the stands at the end of the first circuit. There were loose horses around but no dramas at the Chair fence like last year, and going out away from the stands the pattern was set, with Aldaniti in front and Royal Mail coming through to be the biggest threat, with Spartan Missile getting into the race although still some lengths off the leaders.

Becher's, so often a graveyard of the leaders in the Grand National, was navigated with hardly a nod from Aldaniti, as was the Canal Turn, and turning back towards the stands it was clear that the unthinkable was clearly possible, for Royal Mail was hardly going and Spartan Missile still had some running to do.

Aldaniti gave the third last a clout and although he still looked in command it was then that the ultimate test of the rider's strength and horse's endurance was to come, for Aldaniti had suffered such bad leg problems over the years that he has only run twice in two seasons and such a preparation seemed sure to be too light for those final endless 494 yards of the run-in.

By the last fence Aldaniti still had a length advantage over Royal Mail, and if he seemed marginally less weary than his rival, Spartan Missile and John Thorne were working their way back at them and up that long stretch, so that supporters of sporting dreams hardly knew whom to cheer for, the cancer victim and his former invalid mount or a 54-year-old grandfather who shed two stone in weight to ride the horse he bred and trains himself in Warwickshire.

Royal Mail had kept on to be three lengths away third after a brilliant ride from Philip Blacker. Three to One was fourth and Senator Maclacury fifth of twelve finishers, who sadly did not include the only woman, Linda Sheedy, whose mare Deiopea refused at the 19th, the 44-year-old Manchester solicitor John Carden, who went at the fourth, the oil rig worker Peter Duggan, who refused at the 12th and remounted only to refuse again at the 15th.

Yet in truth the Sun Grand National was only a good luck story. No praise can be too high for the way in which trainer Josh Gifford has kept faith with both his horse and rider. Aldaniti has broken down twice and also broken a bone in his hock. Josh admitted yesterday that he thought owner Nick Embiricos "was crackers to even try and run the horse again after his last breakdown." And although he was unwavering in his promises at Champion's sickbed, privately he admitted that he never considered Bob likely to ride again, or even leave hospital with any reasonable prospect of life ahead.

Bob Champion had his cancer first diagnosed in July of 1979; he had one testicle and a rib removed by surgery and had to undergo intensive chemo-therapy, leaving hospital for the last time on 1 January last year.

The road back has been steady but has had at least two major crises, the continuing battle with his weight (most patients of this therapy put on at least a stone, and Bob has had to keep to a drastic regime of spartan rationing and lengthy sauna sessions to keep his weight at 11 stone), and when he began to ride races again this season the winners were slow to come and the doubters took some convincing.

Indeed, the mind goes back to one afternoon at Fontwell last December when the game almost seemed gone beyond recall. Horses had been falling, other jockeys had begun to take his rides and then Bob took a heavy crash on the flat in one race and was too shaken to ride the winner of the last.

We had a drink in the little open bar beside the track, he grimaced as he moved an injured shoulder and muttered wistfully, "It's very hard at the moment, but I am determined to go on."

Two big winners at Ascot a week later suddenly changed the wheel and since then all the old flair has come back with Aldaniti his 35th winner.

Yesterday's triumph was the greatest sporting tribute to the principle that the battle is never over while the mind is strong.

Aintree's right to claim to be the centre of the world for just one Saturday each spring has never been better demonstrated than this time round, when the sun came out and Bob Champion won the Grand National on Aldaniti.

That was such a day that they even made a smashing film about it, Champions, *with John Hurt in the lead and our now-retired hero in the heavy role of "technical adviser". Yet we don't always get happy endings and that's why I like this piece about Shergar's "King George" at Ascot in July 1981. It might have been his day of triumph but earlier in the week the scene hadn't been quite so smart. Now read on . . .*

Fleeting Doubts—then Swinburn goes for his gun
July 26th 1981

It lasted about ten seconds. Ten of the longest seconds of this horse racing year. The field for the £180,000 King George VI and Queen Elizabeth Diamond Stakes hurtled towards Ascot's final turn and Shergar, trapped in behind the leaders, looked to have nowhere to go.

At last all the talk of multi-million dollar valuations, stud fees and insurance quotes were forgotten. This finally was a real horse race asking a real and vital

Shergar's last victory. Walter Swinburn pats his champion as they come home at Ascot in July 1981 (Chris Smith)

question. Could the dual Derby winner, so clearly superior to his contemporaries, take this first test against his elders? And could he and his nineteen-year-old rider, Walter Swinburn, have the guts as well as the brilliance to work their way out of this most classic of racing dilemmas, the pocket on the rails?

Well, the history books will show that they did. That Shergar had four solid lengths to spare over the French Oaks winner Madam Gay, who had a short head in her favour over Fingal's Cave, with gallant old Master Willie two further lengths back in fourth.

But no one afterwards was pretending this had been anything other than the toughest task Shergar has faced this year, and even sour grapes who, like me, couldn't stump up a quarter of a million quid for a share, have to admit that the bay colt with the big white blaze on his face is as brave as he is good.

Most of all, the problems were for Swinburn. Light Cavalry set only a fair pace, the final time was a moderate 2 minutes 35.40 seconds for the mile and a half and as Master Willie kicked on round the final turn Greville Starkey on Madam Gay was doing no favours to Swinburn and Shergar inside him. But champions of the future don't grow up by asking for quarter and as he walked out for his next ride half an hour later Walter just said: "It was a bit tight for a while but I was always going well enough to feel I could take a gap when one came."

He was the man in the saddle, we just the worriers in the stand, and as the field straightened up for home he got the one gift all jockeys pray for. Light Cavalry, clearly not happy on his suspect foreleg, rolled away from the rails. The gap was there and through it this remarkable nineteen-year-old drove Shergar as if all the Aga Khans in history had ganged up behind him.

This was no effortless surge to match the brilliance of Nijinsky back in 1970 but it was a determined flat-to-the-boards playing of the ace of which any of the previous thirty winners of this great race would be proud.

Afterwards there were those who would argue how lucky it was that Light Cavalry didn't come back on the inside; certainly the much fancied Pelerin got badly put into the rails so that jockey Brian Taylor came back with paint on his boot. But all this didn't matter; Shergar had been put to the test and magnificently had passed.

Much has been made about the astonishing value attached to Shergar's flashing hooves. Of how the Aga Khan has assessed him wonderfully "cheap" at £10m and of how, following the reported sale of last year's top two-year-old, this year's non-runner, Storm Bird, for £16m, the Aga could easily double his price for the colt he bred himself in County Kildare and from whom he so clearly gets as much pleasure as profit. Yesterday was more important for the action than the avarice.

For the prospect of seeing Shergar put to the line had brought a quite enormous crowd to Ascot and they can have only been inspired by what they had seen. This seemed particularly relevant on Saturday for only the day before many of us had made the sad little pilgrimage to Lewisham Crematorium to pay our last respects to Joe Blanks, Ryan Price's young jockey, who never recovered from his horrific fall at Brighton early in the month.

Joe had never scaled the heights young Swinburn surveys today but the son of Ken Blanks, a London taxi driver, had made himself into a thoroughly competent young rider. What's more, he had won many friends by the generosity and gladness of his personality. He had sniffed the heady wind that days like yesterday give off. He had answered the call which many men take from this, and he had paid the highest price.

Young Walter Swinburn, a son of a champion jockey, knows all about that call, and yesterday could hardly believe his good fortune. For even before Shergar's great moment he had ridden the two-year-old filly Circus Ring to a devastating success in the Princess Margaret Stakes—another significant triumph for Shergar's trainer, Michael Stoute.

But there is no doubt that the day was Shergar's. He goes on with already record British earnings of over £400,000 in this one season—which will be closed with a final appearance in the Arc de Triomphe at Longchamp before retiring to the sultan's life at stud.

All congratulations to his connections who have kept him at such a notable peak. They have done much more than that too. They have produced the star on a day which showed that for all its innate absurdities, this game can still be worth the candle.

That race at Ascot was billed as our richest ever run. Six weeks later the story takes us across the Atlantic to the mid-west and for the first time, a million dollars on the wire.

The Shoe slips John Henry a Million
September 6th 1981

You've got to believe it wasn't rigged. Even on the third replay, the whistles and jeers from Arlington Park's betting halls showed what the horse players thought. But there it was on the photo-finish print of last Sunday's Arlington Million in Chicago. This richest ever thoroughbred race had, in the very last breath, been won as expected by the world's most successful six-year-old, ridden by Bill Shoemaker, the winning-most jockey the globe has seen.

So, not for the first time, the actors made the play. All the problems bedevilling this first staging of The Million—the dearth of overseas runners, the over-pricing which led to a disappointingly sparse 28,000 crowd, the Noah's Ark-type deluges which threatened to float the whole project away—were forgotten as the twelve runners combined to produce a truly dramatic horse race with the sort of climax ("Californian living legend beats ex-Irish moke, with British hope third") that belongs to the comic, rather than the photo-finish, strip.

Shoemaker must take the first bow. It's a small one, of course, because to say that Bill lacks inches is to say that Tom Thumb was shortish. On the purpose-built winner's rostrum (tractored into centre stage immediately after The Million), Shoemaker's head was so embarrassingly close to the trophy ledge that he looked like a child peering over a sweet counter. But physique is the only little thing about the man, and never before had this observer so clearly seen the genius which has brought this amazing fifty-year-old a record 8,050 winners, twice as many as Lester Piggott.

For despite John Henry's 26 previous victories, and over a million dollars' worth of prize-money, things were stacked against "The Shoe" and the 2–1 favourite. The ground was much softer than the old horse is supposed to like, and as he was drawn very wide, there was every chance of his having to travel several lengths farther than the rest of the pack.

The first problem didn't seem insuperable and the second Bill solved with a starting-gate manoeuvre not dissimilar to the sort you'd use on a speedbike in a traffic jam. But the real beauty came in the 300-yard straight, The Bart heading for home, Madam Gay unable to do any more despite the most flawless of rides from Piggott, John Henry edged clear and, fired like an arrow by his diminutive pilot, collected right on the wire with the inevitability of greatness.

In the best Shakespearean tradition, this climax was followed by a spot of unintentional knockabout comedy. The dirt track on which the winner's rostrum had been parked so deeply lived up to its name that anyone trying to reach the dais had to go barefoot for fear of losing shoes in the mire. Eventually about 100 people lined up for the formalities.

So John Henry took his winnings to an incredible two-and-a-half million dollars, second only to the extraordinary Spectacular Bid. He might even catch up, because his connections are prepared to campaign him anywhere East or

West. His next objective will probably be the $700,000 Japan Cup in Tokyo, and he would certainly be sent over to take on Shergar and others in the Arc if it were not for the absurd and outdated rule banning geldings. It is a major block on any European race-track trying to echo the inspired enterprise of Arlington.

Those who suggest that he, like most of last Sunday's field, would also be banned after the post-Arc dope test, fail to understand the horse and his circumstances.

Horses like John Henry run on Butazolidin, not because they are congenitally unsound, but to enable them to survive the rigours of the American dirt racing tracks. Few British trainers would even trot a horse on the hard-based slop. I cantered round on Sunday morning, and decided that John Henry, who hadn't been using Butazolidin back at his drier Californian base, could not have survived sixty races on dirt tracks without having legs of iron. He would find the European surfaces a pile carpet by comparison.

John Henry is also one of the great originals. Back at the barn on Sunday he was being led round by his dapper Puerto Rican handler, Louis Cenicola. "In the mornings he doesn't bother himself," said Louis. "But when he goes to the race track he's something else. He always thinks he's won."

As Louis began to hose down his lean and angular champion, the mind went back to another recovery barn and another old gelding whose exploits made him a hero to a nation. Louis even used the same phrase Ginger McCain always bestowed on his beloved Red Rum: "He's an old pro."

The John Henry story continued on its amazing way and by the time he took the Golden Gates Handicap in San Francisco in May 1984 (his 25th Stakes race) he had hoisted his winnings to a record $4,481,000. The sun doesn't always shine as it has done on John Henry. But if bad weather can sometimes make the watching pretty unbearable, it doesn't necessarily detract from the drama. Witness this report from Newmarket in October 1983, when mighty winds blew and to be a jockey required an advanced degree in navigation. How did Steve Cauthen learn that in landlocked Kentucky?

Cauthen Champion Masterpiece
October 16th 1983

When Steve Cauthen first blazed to stardom in New York, he was famous for late finishes and known only as "The Kid". He's a man now, but he'll never come later on the scene than he did to win the Champion Stakes on Cormorant Wood at Newmarket yesterday.

Two furlongs from home, Cauthen was plum last of the nine runners with a wall of horses in front of him and a hurricane blowing them all together. To get through at all needed something like a miracle. To manage it and put the filly's head in front right on the line was as near to being a masterpiece as is possible in race-riding.

On any other day, such extreme tactics would have been a reckless gamble, but this was no ordinary day. We had something akin to Typhoon Tommy blowing across the course, and even such a giant of a horse as Salmon Leap got tossed around like a leaf in a storm, and Cormorant Wood, sheltered on the inside, undoubtedly saved priceless energy for her final throw.

It was significant that the three most fancied horses were drawn out on the far side and had to take the brunt of the gale. It was also not surprising that the closing stages were full of incident even before Cormorant Wood stormed through between Tolomeo and the Irish filly, Flame of Tara, in the last fifty yards.

A Stewards' inquiry was called. An objection was announced. Then it became clear that the incident involved Tolomeo's emergence from the pack a furlong-and-a-half out. He was eventually found guilty of impeding the fourth horse, Miramar Reef (a 200–1 outsider), and demoted to that place, with Flame of Tara and Miramar Reef both going up into the winnings.

More than that, Tolomeo's Sardinian rider, Gianfranco Dettori, was given eight days' suspension starting next Sunday, and thereby completes an unhappy big-race double. For Dettori's last English race was in the Epsom Derby, and that also ended in an enforced holiday. Gianfranco is undoubtedly a major force in Italy, but his pea-on-drum riding style seems to give him steering problems over here.

Nonetheless, Tolomeo ran a magnificent race on his first outing since winning the Arlington Million in Chicago in August. And he didn't help his or Dettori's cause by pulling like a runaway tram early on. Flame of Tara too put up a marvellous performance, but Cormorant Wood had to be seen to be believed.

A furlong from home there was one really superb moment. Two hundred yards to go in the richest race ever run at Newmarket. Eighteen horses and jockeys flailing for the line, but then the eye caught the nineteenth, Cormorant Wood, in fifth place, with Cauthen actually pulling her back as he tried to find a route to fire the filly through. Tolomeo and Flame of Tara rolled apart. Cauthen's back flattened. Cormorant Wood stretched. The winning post flashed towards them, but the deed was done. It was as sweet a moment as flat racing ever gives, and the great news afterwards was that both Cormorant Wood and Flame of Tara stay in training to renew battle next season.

If that was drama, in the next race, the Cesarewitch, we had a great finish and tears too. Tears streamed down the face of the winning trainer, Rodney Simpson, as he hugged Bajan Sunshine, his moment of triumph made bitter-sweet by the knowledge that the horse is to leave his stable this week.

For Simpson's Epsom yard is being taken over at the end of this season, and a couple of days ago he sold Bajan Sunshine to the Channel Island entrepreneur, Paul Green. This owner is going to send the horse on to join his other horses at Martin Tate's Worcestershire yard, but he granted Simpson's last wish of running Bajan Sunshine in the Cesarewitch, for which the trainer claimed he was a "certainty".

Such optimism in the face of impending doom deserved the reward, especially in the storm-tossed conditions which must have made this two-and-a-quarter-mile marathon seem almost like Dick Turpin's ride from London to York. Indeed, if not Black Bess, it was another mare, Mayotte, who looked for long as if she was going to triumph. But hard though she struggled, she couldn't handle the double attack of Bajan Sunshine and Popsi's Joy, who had, of course, won under Lester Piggott in 1980, but yesterday young Sean Keightley did nothing wrong as he put in the gallant veteran in front 100 yards out. Unhappily for his backers, the old horse couldn't quite resist Bajan Sunshine's renewed flourish, and those final uphill yards were just beyond him.

Whatever the weather, Newmarket still likes to call itself the "Headquarters" of the racing game and to ride a big winner there means a jockey has really arrived. The journey towards such coveted circles is attempted by thousands of youngsters every year. Not many make it, but here's a story of one who might . . . and by a fairly unusual route.

The Miniature Magic of Quinn the Uncatchable
November 6th 1983

It's not often that you see the future made flesh. But it happened with Richard Quinn in Munich on Tuesday. He left the paddock a child, and came back a man.

That's perhaps brushing aside the achievements, including 60-odd winners that this little Scottish apprentice has already packed into the 21 years since he was born the first of eight children in a council house near Bannockburn. Yet with the sun already set somewhere over Switzerland, young Richard looked much more the cheeky kid than the seasoned professional as he cantered out into the Bavarian gloom for this tenth and last race of the day.

It was the final event in the German leg of the European Apprentice Championship (sponsored generously, if a shade inappropriately, by Long John Scotch Whisky), and the eight riders so perfectly fitted their national stereotypes that you could have been looking at a Unicef poster. Among them was a glamorous, long-haired Italian called Marco Paganini, a lovely blonde Swedish girl named Pia Johannson, a gloriously craggy-faced Irish boy called Pat Shanahan and, from Spain, an incorrigible, dark-skinned little lad named Augustin Lopes who looked as if he should have been running barefoot after the bulls. (He once enlivened a dull official dinner in Paris by crawling under the table and disappearing into the night to spend a couple of hours on the Eiffel Tower.)

It was getting cold in Munich, but you had to warm to the stories of this Lilliputian circus come to town. Lopes, whose head can't have reached over his brother's bar at Madrid race-course when at thirteen he was dispatched to stable life. Shanahan, who weighed only 3st 3lb when he started his seven years of pony racing in Ireland at the tender age of eight. And Quinn himself, who had to sleep three to a bed with his younger brothers, and whose first racing experiences were with the iron-mouthed trotters who used to pound round the stadium at Corbie Wood, near Stirling.

Sheer size, or lack of it, had put them on the road to Munich, and to get thus far meant that they had already climbed over the sad, scrabbling heap of little kids who also dreamed the jockey's dream, and were set to slave all hours to land it.

Conditions in British stables aren't always far removed from a Dickensian nightmare, and a new British racing school at Newmarket for young hopefuls won't be officially opened until the end of the month. But the conditions, as well as the incentive of the system (we are the only country in Europe where the trainer can take half an apprentice's earnings), mean that those who get through are a match for anyone.

Quinn has clearly proved this point over the fourteen races of this European Championship, which ended at Doncaster yesterday. Even before he got to Munich, Richard had built up a 47-point lead with victories in Sweden, Denmark and Italy (this last earning him the local tag of "Piccolo Piggott"), and it seemed that only a severe case of swollen head or diabolical luck in the draw for horses could prevent the Piccolo Piggott staying in front.

So the would-be wonder boy whose father now drives a taxi in Willie Carson's home town of Stirling was very much on trial on Tuesday, particularly as students of Munich form assured us that Quinn had drawn moderate mounts in the ballot. What's more, some of us had still to be convinced that Quinn was much more than a lucky, and sometimes slightly stick-happy, young boy.

First portents weren't good, for Richard could finish only sixth in the opening event, but two straws in the wind suggested a successful outcome. First the fact that, although universally unpopular with the young jockeys, the riders were allowed only a stunted twelve-inch whip, and second our hero's calm statement, "Of course it's going to be long and hard, especially after I lose the claim (apprentice's weight allowance), but I'm going to try. We're all here to learn."

Out on the track, the most crucial learning process is how to get individual horses to run. To do this consistently when logic and previous form defy you is the absolute criterion of talent. In Munich, Richard first showed this ability in the second round when he almost got home on an unwilling-looking beast called Flower des Alpes to collect enough points to make a great effort on the supposedly unfancied Sire unnecessary in the last.

If you really want to study a jockey (or any sportsman for that matter) nothing beats getting really close to the action at ground level. In Munich on Tuesday, this meant pushing through those green coats, alpine hats and shepherd dogs on leads that make up the German race crowd. Quinn had Sire settled in third place on the rails, the pole position stars seem to get by right. Two furlongs out, the horse had run above expectations to be still third as the French and Irish apprentices duelled in the lead.

Then the moment of brilliance. Quinn switched his horse to the middle of the track, and in twenty strides of complete mental and physical inspiration, one tiny athlete galvanised a much larger one to stretch out and pass his rivals. When Richard rode back, the serenity of his smile was as old as victory itself. After all, he had not just clinched the championship—if he keeps his head, he has booked himself a ticket for life.

Quinn has it all before him and he started off well in 1984.
Now this chapter has to close and indeed this book had to
be put to bed by the beginning of May. So what happened
at Sandown on 28th April was timed to the minute. Maybe
it wasn't set up by the great editor in the sky, but it
certainly made you suspicious.

Her Majesty's Pleasure
April 29th 1984

It was as near as we'll get to the ultimate horse race. Three-and-a-half miles travelled, 24 fences crossed, four brave horses straining up the Sandown hill for a double photo-finish, with victory finally going to jump racing's best-loved colours, the blue and buff silks of Queen Elizabeth the Queen Mother.

This Whitbread Gold Cup was the royal lady's biggest success as an owner, and some repayment for her many years' devotion to the jumping game. But it was much more than that. It was final proof that within the confines of a horse race you can sometimes experience enough twist on the emotions to make any script-writer blush.

Each of the first four home deserves a chapter to himself. The winner, Special Cargo, came from an impossible position two fences out, and from two years lameness before that. The second, Lettoch, came from being almost knocked over after half a mile. The third, Diamond Edge, came within two short heads of a record third Whitbread and, in fourth place, Plundering came within two lengths of finally laying the hoodoo that has haunted Fred Winter as jockey and trainer in this race.

The stories go on. Special Cargo was an unprecedented seventh Whitbread victory for 73-year-old Fulke Walwyn, who also saddled the thirteen-year-old

Diamond Edge, on whom Special Cargo's regular jockey Bill Smith, was making a magnificent, if heartbreaking, final appearance. Lettoch's trainer, Michael Dickinson, is also quitting the National Hunt scene after the most meteoric career in the game, and if Plundering had collected, Winter would have won the season's long duel with Dickinson for the trainer's title.

But on to the race, under brilliant spring sky and before a huge crowd who spent the rest of the afternoon with such flat-racing delights as a Derby trial and a controversial Lester Piggott double. He was disqualified in the fifth, and then landed a last-stride victory in the sixth. Don't let's decry Piggott's adventures, which brought him a five-day suspension, or Alphabatim's brave run in the Guardian Classic Trial. It's just that this time they had to take second billing to the last big steeplechase as Diamond Edge and Bill Smith led the fifteen-runner Whitbread field out into the country.

No thirteen-year-old has ever even been placed in the Whitbread, but Diamond Edge didn't win his two previous Gold Cups by reading the Form book, and his forceful young man's gallop soon had his two least experienced rivals in trouble. At the downhill third fence, Donegal Prince misjudged the drop, and in avoiding him Lettoch lost at least a dozen lengths.

The rest of this first exploratory circuit continued uneventfully, so that as Ashley House and Plundering came to test Diamond Edge down the back stretch, we knew that fireworks were bound to happen. The fences come at you very quickly off the turn—two plain ones, then an open ditch, a run on over the water jump, then three more quick ones before the homeward climb.

Seven times the young challengers pushed up to match strides with the old champion. Seven times Diamond Edge saw them off, only then to give way like some ageing stag as Plundering and Ashley House pressed on towards the Pond fence three from the finish. At this stage Lettoch was the clear danger to the leading pair, and only their loyallest supporters could have really fancied either Diamond Edge to throw off the years or, further back, for his stable companion, Special Cargo, to put spring into his battered old legs as Kevin Mooney urged him forward.

Crossing the second last, Lettoch had taken over, and as Plundering raced with him, the stage seemed set for the expected Dickinson-Winter trainers' duel. One fence to go, and it was desperate stuff.

Plundering was the first to crack, rolling away to Lettoch's left and leaving a gap through which Bill Smith drove Diamond Edge with the knowledge that this was the absolute final throw for horse and rider. A hundred yards to go, and Diamond Edge was only a neck down and gaining. But now another twist. Special Cargo was within two lengths and Kevin Mooney had him flying.

All three were together as the post flashed by. First thoughts were that none could be a loser. A few minutes later, when Special Cargo's name had been called and his owner stood in the victory circle, her pale blue coat matching Mooney's silks, you had to think that perhaps we had the right result.

2.The Players

In many ways jockeys have the best life in the world. Those words are written with all the wistful nostalgia of an ex-jock who now has a whole decade between him and the pigskin days. That's why you might detect a touch of envy in this little gallery overleaf. But there's also some admiration, sympathy and even the occasional drop of awe. After all, whatever abuse we may occasionally want to hurl at them, the jockeys are the guys (and the gals) in the saddle. I am here to tell you that it ain't always that easy . . . and I have the scars to prove it.

Let's start in the summer of '74, and spend a long, long day with Willie Carson who had been the flat-race champion in '72 and '73.

An Exhausting Day with Willie Carson
July 14th 1974

07.25   The big gold Mercedes comes whirling up the drive. Willie Carson's face, still crumpled with sleep, lights into an irrepressible schoolboy grin as he meets trainer Barry Hills. It is the start of busiest week yet in Carson's relentless battle to retain his crown. By the end of the week Carson will have had fifty rides in six afternoon and four evening meetings. Monday brings simple delights of racing at Pontefract and Wolverhampton.

07.57   Whispering hoof-beats, straining horses and trainer Hills's intent eyes as Carson leads the morning work-outs over a specially prepared sawdust strip on Lambourn Downs. After one gallop, Carson returns for the next, his face transformed from that of a happy little terrier into the high cheekboned determination of a professional gunman. He rides out for a full hour, finally sitting motionless above the withers of Dibidale, his fifth horse of the morning. In the hot sun Dibidale is now having to cross undulating turf gallops complete with saddle-anchoring breast-girth. She would have won the Oaks but for a slipping saddle. We are now half way through the season: Carson has had one solitary day off in three months—and that when racing was cancelled. Riding out and racing, in England and the Continent, occupies seven days a week.

Overleaf: Race for the line in the 1984 Craven Stakes at Newmarket. Greville Starkey (left) on Lear Fan and Steve Cauthen on Rainbow Quest (Chris Smith)

09.30   While others feast on the boundless Hills breakfast hospitality, Carson bounces in after phoning his secretary to arrange travel and scheduling. "Marvellous!" he says. "Lightest ride is eight stone one—let's have some breakfast." Bacon and eggs compare with the less substantial morning ration of coffee and toast to which he reverts next day to meet the scales at 7st 8lb. Overnight, too, his Monday plans had changed from riding the evening meeting at Windsor to the longer journey to Wolverhampton.

Willie's day. Top:
the gallops and
breakfast; centre: the
scales, the flight, the
race; left: nightcap
(sequence: Gerry
Cranham)

12.15   Newbury airstrip, ready to fly to Pontefract. Carson asleep within five minutes. Over South Yorkshire chimneys and slagheaps, land Doncaster at 1.20 pm. Taxi called "Dog" to complete fifteen miles to Ponty. Dog does the dirty. Flat tyre. Half-hour wait. Second taxi. Worse than Cresta Run: driver last of Hell Drivers. Still arrive late: Carson misses 2.45 race.

14.55   On the scales. He will go there a hundred times during the week. Time always desperately short. Saddles, lead cloths and pads have to be changed and adjusted for the right weight. Different horses need special equipment such as blinkers or breast-plates. All have to be checked by the valets. All equipment has to be gathered and carried on to the scales within minutes of the previous ride. The valets are scrabbling with leads and buckles, jockeys go through the process in a state of semi-automation, often calling out: "What weight? What weight?" Carson is twice champion jockey: in the weighing-room it counts for nothing.

15.15   Carson's first ride at Pontefract. The course is all hot Yorkshire shirt-sleeved sense of humour, and racing has actually been cancelled on occasion because of subsidence into the disused pit-shafts beneath. Hula Hula, Carson's ride here (No 2), starts second favourite at evens. First out of the stalls, they lead for three furlongs in a mile race. But, for all his pushing, the champion never lets up, Hula Hula can only finish third. "I tried to slow the field down early on," he explains. "But she just didn't seem to get the trip at all." Always the animals are talked of like people; not softly, but as if they were business clients. His second mount, Knockers, ran second in the 3.45. For the first time in the day there is an annoyed edge in his voice: "I should have won there. Jock Skilling's horse (Uncle Vanya—unplaced) rolled all over me three furlongs out."

16.30   Airborne again, heading for Wolverhampton, garden suburb one minute, straggling slum the next. Coffee, but no food, and Carson sleeps during the 45-minute flight. His success is founded on appetite for work: last year he rode 883 times for 163 winners; this year he may top the thousand.

18.15   Wolverhampton. First ride is Willow Song, first daughter of the famous Park Top. Equally famous straw-coloured silks of Duke of Devonshire. Carson gets another good start, but finishes "in the middle" although the horse "ran better than her previous race." The race-winner, Pat Eddery, goes five winners ahead in championship. Eddery has led Carson all season. They leave weighing-room together, joking. But does Carson worry about rival? "Oh yes, I want to be champion. But Pat's doing really well at the moment."

20.20   Carson's turn to go well. Wins the 8.10 on Redesdale, and then talks with trainer Bernard van Cutsem, who helped establish him. After Wolverhampton, driven home by Ted Eley, his race secretary. Eley booked for motorway speeding. Carson grudgingly eats steak, motorway shandy ("I'll have to sweat tomorrow") and sleeps in car.

01.15   Back at Falmouth Cottage, Victorian house in Newmarket which goes with the job of Lord Derby's jockey. Lord Derby and van Cutsem have first claim on Carson. Still no relaxation; still no sign of edginess from the little man. In his office, a large white board lists the meetings and rides for the week. Carson and Eley add the day's bookings, and listen to messages on telephone answering machine. Sipping whisky Carson begins to study the next day's card. I recall something Ted Eley said earlier in the day: "My little fella's only just getting going. He breaks the others' hearts. Pat Eddery will be dead by the end of August." Writer and photographer decide we don't want to be champion jockeys.

*All that effort was to no avail. Pat Eddery couldn't be
killed off and in fact won the title for the next four seasons.
Nonetheless Willie got it back again in 1978 and 1980 and
has become something of a national hero by the time he
appears again later in the chapter.
A contrast now . . . Ron Barry, the National Hunt
champion between 1972 and 1974 and a man so big and
strong you felt he could probably eat Carson for breakfast
and then look around for another piece of toast.*

Ron Barry at Large
November 29th 1979

It is typical of what is best in jump racing, and in its champion Ron Barry, who yesterday rode The Dikler into a promising fifth place in the Massey Ferguson Gold Cup, that nobody bothered very much about his physical achievement in riding at Cheltenham at all.

For he was riding with one arm in plaster from a fall at Wetherby three weeks ago which broke two bones in his left hand and one in the wrist. And riding the massive bay bulk of The Dikler down to the start, and in the early part of the race, is like trying to steady a ten-ton truck down Cleeve Hill with a faulty handbrake.

Of course, the 6ft, 31-year-old Irishman is no stranger to achievement, having set a record of 125 winners in a season in 1973, and easily retained his title last year. But from bare statistics you could doubt whether the blade is quite as sharp this season—only nineteen winners so far, eleven adrift of the leader, Tommy Stack, and two behind the talented Jonjo O'Neill, his understudy at Gordon Richards's stable in Cumberland. He also got married last summer to the bright and charming Liz Young, so it may be legitimate to ask whether the lifestyle, as well as the bones, is getting a little soft.

He picked us up just after half-past seven last Tuesday morning. The light was creeping up on Ullswater, and the first impression as he kicked the big Audi out through the gates and away from the lake was that, apart from anything else, his head was still pretty strong. For travelling problems the night before which delayed our arrival had certainly not dampened our welcome. Yet if the big Robert Mitchum face looked a bit more crumpled, and the deep Limerick brogue sounded thicker than ever, there wasn't much wrong with the reactions as we swerved round a stray farmer in the gloom.

Nor was there much nervousness about the hand on the end of the plaster cast, since he continued to light a cigarette with it as we made this manoeuvre. But then, seeing the racing world through Ron Barry's eyes, there is not much to be nervous about. "Ah, the hand's great really," he said as we swept up to Gordon Richards's happy and successful yard centred around the old coaching stables of Greystoke Castle, "but it was a bad fall, mind. I asked him to take off at the last, and he didn't get there. Put his foot through the top like. Nasty."

A clinical explanation, and then a big soft laugh. That's Ron Barry, supremely good at his job but very relaxed about it. Like a big friendly Labrador. That morning (which was beautiful) and the next (as raw and freezing as the snow up on the distant Saddleback Fell), he went through the whole gamut of the training scene. Trotting, cantering, galloping and jumping. Always easily in control, and most of the time buoying the others up with his nudging Irish humour.

The return to race riding came on Wednesday afternoon at an Ayr whose famous balmy climate had given way to Siberian showers. Four rides, no winners, but one moment in the novice 'chase that showed the quality. The promising but fallible Sedge Warbler got much too close, and clouted the first fence in the back straight. His weight and balance pitched down, but Barry held him. A man less strong, less poised, less confident, could have let the horse go. Afterwards many jockeys would have dramatised with X-certificate stories. For Barry, big boxer's body on long runner's legs: "Ah, it was nothing . . ."

Next day, through the vicarious excitement of the betting-shop commentary, I heard him get Greystoke Rambler home in a photo-finish. It was the five hundredth winner of a career which started thirteen years ago when the 6st 5lb apprentice kidded the funny-tempered Lluvia to win at Gowran Park.

Will this be the start of a charge up the jockeys' table? "I'll have a right go," he says, "but Stacky is a long way in front, and I have got to get up there first."

Other jockeys are as brave, but none as strong and relaxed. At 5–1 he is very good value for the title. For if you had to select a team to storm some present-day Guns of Navarone, this man would be the first on the list.

*Big Ron didn't make the championship again but he
continued on, his skills and his massively strong body still
wonderfully intact, right through to the Autumn of 1983.
His last ride was a winner, on the appropriately named*

Final Argument at Ayr on October 15th. It was Ron
Barry's 923rd winner. He said afterwards, "It's a great life
if you don't weaken. I've weakened." But the affection in
which he was held was shown by his being the first jockey
ever to be awarded a Benefit Year.
Across the channel next and to the one jockey who has
always had superstar status over there. The man some
French racegoers reverently call "Monsieur" St Martin.

Very Cool, Very Yves
April 25th 1976

For a man who spent last Sunday in hospital, and last week nursing torn back muscles and a dizzy head, Yves St Martin is quite calm about this week's prospects, which merely include flying over to Newmarket and annexing the first two English classics for France with Manado and Flying Water.

"The horses are very well," he says, "and I am in form." That ought to be enough from the man who won the 1974 Arc de Triomphe on Allez France between hospital sessions on a badly damaged hip. Yet as always, only winners will prevent the 34-year-old French champion being dismissed by chauvinistically disgruntled punters as a "useless Frog".

For although St Martin has won every English classic bar the St Leger, and took the first of them fourteen years ago, he is still little more than the French ace with the film-star looks to most people. In reality, he has long become one of the outstanding, not to mention highest paid, figures in European sport, having first become French champion jockey as a nineteen-year-old apprentice in 1960, and won that coveted Cravache d'Or for a record twelfth time last season.

With more than 150 winners a year, and the lucrative Wildenstein retainer, St Martin's annual earnings are well into six figures, and a visit to his lovely new home set in the Forêt du Lys just south of Chantilly speaks well of the fruits of success. But the extraordinary quality of this man is that he has not allowed this wealth to cloy either his talents or his personality—finding someone who dislikes St Martin is more difficult than getting buyers for the pound. Perhaps it is just natural self-possession. He walks into the luxuriously-appointed living room barelegged in a cream towelling robe ready for the sauna. He talks happily about his skiing holiday (January is the only full month clear of riding), of his wife and family, of his farm in Aquitaine, and to the hammy old question, "What's your secret?" answers with disarming gentleness: "I always have confidence in my own ability, and before a big race I am very cool."

Perhaps it is the inbuilt survival sense of a man who weighed only 2¾lb when he was born to a prison warder's wife at Agen, Bordeaux, who fell off his first racecourse ride, and who suffered the miseries of bedwetting as a teenage apprentice.

Out on the course, there is plenty of evidence of the calm and the urgency—the calm in his generalship through a race ("Yves knows what he is doing, knows where he is going," says Lester Piggott appreciatively) and the urgency in his finishing drive. But above these assets there is something else to the secret of St Martin. It comes through when he talks of his dogs, of his prize-winning cattle and of the great horses he has ridden. It is a quality that Lester Piggott (like him an only son) shares in a different way, and it is the easier-talking St Martin who puts it best into words. "All my life," he says, with those big dark eyes lighting up from their heavy look of concentration, "I have had a great affinity with animals. With horses, I like to get to know them and help them in a race."

St Martin was the star of my first—and most catastrophic so far—TV interview. Before he went out to win the 1971 One Thousand Guineas on Altesse Royale, I produced an amazing scoop—a chat with our cross-Channel wizard on the box. He spoke graciously and well, and said he would nearly win (at 25–1, no less!). But to my dismay, and the producer's increasing apoplexy, such goodies were only for the linguists among the viewers. Every word was in French.

Five days after this was written Yves was again chattering away at Newmarket. He had pronounced himself fit enough to steer little Flying Water to a brilliant victory in the One Thousand Guineas. It was proof that champions are made to conquer pain even if he hadn't been as far down as our next story . . . March 1978 and champion jump jockey Tommy Stack is at the end of a very, long, hard, haul.

Tommy Stack on the Rack
March 5th 1978

It happened at Hexham just six months, half-a-year, ago today. For Tommy Stack, it has been like half a lifetime. The accident was quick and brutal. As he landed in the saddle for his last ride of the day, his horse reared straight over backwards, pinning him to the paddock tarmac. More than one hardened Northumbrian observer turned away muttering: "That's a dead 'un for sure."

Stack was not dead, unconscious, or even paralysed. "I could wiggle my toes." But his situation was still desperate by any normal standards. His pelvis was badly crushed and displaced, his bladder damaged and the ambulance drive along the bumpy hilltop road back towards the town was a torture unpleasant to contemplate even now.

The next stage was an updated 74-day version of the rack, and Stack's career looked surely threatened. In the fourteen years since he had come over from his native Ireland, he had grafted his way up the tree, finally to take the jump jockeys championship in 1975. By the time he regained it from John Francome last year he had become a household name with his record-breaking Grand National win on Red Rum. That all seemed far away as most visitors to Hexham's magnificent hospital echoed the first medical opinion that Stack would be lucky to ride again this season, if ever.

As one doctor said later: "I told him we would get him fit to ride Red Rum in the National on 1 April, but, quite honestly, at that stage it was more to give him hope than being realistic."

That he has already ridden and had two other rides besides Red Rum yesterday, could be called a miracle—even though there is a further bladder operation this week. But the word miracle seeks to avoid an explanation which is not hard to find. For Stack is a champion in one of the most demanding sports of all. He has had to do his share of battening down the hatches of the mind when the going gets rough, and those are just the qualities that were needed in his ordeal.

He summed it up one night last October: "I've had six weeks so far. Another six to go. It's like riding a bad jumper in a three-mile chase at Wetherby. We've done one circuit, and we've got to go out into the country again."

September

The Rack. Stack's pelvis was severely crushed, and his bladder damaged. On the first evening he had over two stones on the left leg, and was X-rayed every half-hour as they tried to pull the pelvis into line. After that it was a mere stone-and-a-half on the left leg, a stone on the right and the intermittent torture of a tube in the bladder. He stayed like this from 5 September to 28 November.

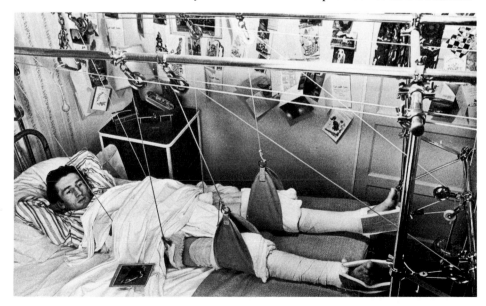

Wired up for twelve weeks. Tommy Stack, October 1977 (Chris Smith)

November

The whipcord ten-stone jockey was reduced to a painful eight stone by the time he was cut down. "I had no appetite. It was like trying to push your food uphill." His hips and legs were lowered on successive days. A full day was spent lying flat but the moment they tried to stand him up he passed clean out. "It was like someone pouring a huge bucket of hot blood down my legs." The swimming pool could at least provide him with supported movement.

December

Leaving hospital. Despite the smile, this was the worst period of all: "Somehow I felt after all that time everything would be all right once I got home. But I could only just walk, couldn't even dress myself and could do nothing else at all. I have never felt so helpless in all my life." At their brightly decorated farmhouse near Tadcaster, Liz Stack remembers vividly: "He seemed desperately tired. He would just keep falling to sleep for no reason."

January

The long grind to fitness. Stack checked into the Sports Medicine Unit at Leeds Hospital when he got home, but was so weak that he could not start the exercises until the New Year. Soon he was doing an hour-and-a-half circuit training a day, and besides the bicycle and rowing machine there was a progression of weights and exercises that gradually restored his vitality and weight.

February

He didn't plan to ride a racehorse until the following Thursday, but he got legged

up on Scatter, his neighbour's pony, four days early. Since then, he has been riding out four hours a day with a local trainer Peter Asquith, riding progressively short to develop his thigh muscles. He rode Red Rum in a gallop on 23 February, had his first practice jump the next day and his first ride at Doncaster on the 27th.

March

Tommy Stack and Red Rum were reunited at Haydock yesterday. They finished sixth—27 lengths behind Rambling Artist, winner of the Greenall Whitley Chase—after nearly parting company at the 12th fence. Tommy, obviously relieved to have survived Red Rum's uncharacteristic blunder, said: "He ran as well as I expected and was staying on at the finish." Referring to his own battered frame, Tommy added: "I feel fine."

The dream of a second National victory never materialised because Red Rum went lame a week before the great race. However the big fight back to fitness was not wasted because in April Stack won the Whitbread Gold Cup on Strombolus and that summer retired to manage the Longfield stud, part of the Vincent O'Brien empire in Ireland. It's an irony that for all the injuries accumulated

above, Stack's worst moment came after he quit the saddle.
Out in the field a playful colt kicked out, fractured
Tommy's skull and damn near killed him. Sometimes it's
just the life-style that catches you.
Here's Graham Thorner in December '79.

Retirement at Thirty—a Merciful Release
December 23rd 1979

If you have ever driven a car with the choke out, you will know what it was like to be a horse ridden by Graham Thorner. You might also understand why, at only thirty, he is such a pale, emaciated wreck of the champion he once was, and that the announcement of his retirement was universally welcomed. For although seven riders have totalled more than Thorner's 650 winners, and several have continued longer than his fifteen seasons, no jockey, indeed no sportsman, has put so much of himself on the line.

It is fourteen years since Graham and I drove to Wincanton together. Already quite experienced, I played the uncle to the little Somerset farmer's son who was having his first ride on a race-course. It was very much the concerned uncle, too, for there were lots of runners, and Graham's ride had little ability. To everyone's amazement he had his horse, an old plug called Father Borelli, up with the leaders before fading back where he belonged. For the first of a thousand times we shook our heads and said: "That Thorner can ride a bit."

Surprisingly and significantly, the two first impressions of Graham that day—extraordinary, intense energy, and a certain country-boy simplicity—have endured. His eyes would dilate and his hands clench as he told you of the excitement of the race, and his voice would drop into an awed West Country whisper as he talked of the people of the day.

It was the sort of energy which, grafted on to basic Pony Club horsemanship, was bound to lead to success. We both worked at Tim Forster's stable, where he remained from leaving school until last week.

As the rides became more frequent, I remember him gritting his false teeth (his real ones were smashed on only his sixth ride) and saying: "I know I can beat these other bastards. I won't give best to anyone."

Sure enough, the winners began to flow. Within four seasons he was champion jockey, within five had become the youngest rider to double this feat with a Grand National win, on Well To Do in 1972. All the time that Somerset simplicity, which should never be confused with lack of intelligence, remained his greatest asset as a man, but his final downfall as a jockey.

It meant that he was never bewitched by the siren song of the flashier side of racing. "I love meeting famous people, and going to some of the dos," he used to say, wide-eyed with enjoyment. "But that's not my land. I have got my little farm and a decent life for Caroline and our three girls by grafting like a bastard, not floating around at clubs or chatting up Lord This or Lady That.''

The straightforward approach (''I aim to give not just a hundred per cent, but one hundred and ten per cent'') also meant that as a rider he still drove with the hunger of a contender rather than occasionally allowing himself to coast with the expertise of a champion. Hard to the point of ruthlessness on his horses in the finish (''I like to give them a bit of whang''), he was always harder on himself, and inevitably the ground caught up with him, although on one occasion he wouldn't let even a fall prevent him going for a win. After a three-horse pile-up at the last, he was back on board in a flash, and belabouring the wretched animal past the post. Then he discovered he'd got the wrong horse.

Other incidents did more damage. At one stage he was admitted to hospital with exhaustion, and he escaped few of the fractures and concussions, little of the sheer mud-biting agony of the steeplechasing fall. Most of his bones were broken, but after badly damaging one leg eighteen months ago, he broke the other one last September, and although he was back within weeks he was a strained shadow of himself.

''There has always been pressure,'' says Thorner, ''but if I was well, I could handle it. Then I didn't seem to fit into the horses properly any more. I had some tummy bug, and suddenly I was just burnt out.''

Tim Forster, with whom Thorner had shared an unparalleled four hundred winner partnership, saw the crisis coming, and diplomatically tried to bring it to a head: ''It was awful to see him struggling on with all his usual courage, but obviously in pain. I know how agonising the decision must have been, but I'm sure he's done the right thing. Nobody, and I repeat nobody, has given so much over the years to one stable as he has done.''

At lunch last Wednesday, Thorner was clearly on the mend. ''But I'm glad you saw me last week,'' he said, ''because you saw me bad, saw why I had to stop. I shall find another farm, some more horses, try anything.''

Suddenly you appreciated that he'd finally shed the old, battered jockey skin and you realised how young, eager and bright he was. Ready at thirty for a new life. But don't bank on the choke being in.

Graham certainly hasn't taken to the lazy life and looks as lean now as he did in his riding days. He is installed in an impressive training yard near Wantage and in 1983 won both the Phillip Cornes Final and the Great Yorkshire Chase. Personal involvement always makes stories tricky to write and the next one doubly so. Bob Champion had been a friend through my riding days, and both my parents had died long difficult deaths with cancer. Bob didn't, but sometimes, looking back, it's still hard to believe it.

The Incredible Journey
August 24th 1980

There are many journeys you can make from the cancer ward. A lot are hoped for, one is dreaded. But never before has anyone charted the route Bob Champion completes this week, the voyage from that pit of despair to the highest level of the steeplechasing world.

A year ago, Bob's hold on that or any other existence looked decidedly temporary. Having worked his way up over eleven seasons and some 350 winners to become one of the most respected riders in the game, he had just lost a testicle to remove one growth, half a rib to explore another and, with that diagnosed as malignant, faced the prospect of intensive chemotherapy between him and a certain grave within twelve months.

So six times over the following eighteen weeks, he went into a Surrey hospital to endure five days of intravenous administration of a new three-part combination of drugs including platinum. This is a new chemotherapy treatment which, if only suitable for certain specialised forms of cancer, has a very high success rate, but whose side-effects can make bystanders fear the worst. To see him whey-faced and rapidly balding, and to go through the "Yes, I'll be back in the saddle soon" make-believe, was an experience which drove even a strong man like Josh Gifford to the bottle that he had taken in as a gift. Yet, here we are less than eight months after Bob Champion tottered out of hospital for the last time, welcoming him back not as any fragile convalescent, but as a bronzed young sportsman whose fitness would be the envy of any other 32-year-old in the country.

Before breakfast two weeks ago, I watched Bob ride eight horses two miles each round the sweeping left-handed oval of the Saratoga training track. Last week he had two more race rides to bring his total during his American rehabilitatory summer to nine, including two winners and two falls. "To be honest," he says in that gentle way, "I think I am fitter than I have ever been. I can chase one all the way now, and I could never do that before."

The facts are that since Bob got the all clear at the end of his final hospital treatment last 1 January—"The best New Year's present I will ever have"—he has passed every one of the check-ups, which have to be frequent during the first risky year. It is an extraordinary medical achievement, and the normally reticent Champion is happy now to speak about his ordeal. "If what I've been through can give hope to just one person, then I'll be happy," he said. But there is little doubt that the victory also owes much to his own determination, and to the support of his family and friends.

Chief among these was his sister Mary, whose friendly Wiltshire farmhouse was a haven between treatments. "The first time back was the worst," she recalled on Thursday. "But, except one night later on when he had to be rushed to hospital with septicaemia, I never thought he was actually going to die. He used to look desperately tired, but we didn't want to let him get sorry for himself,

and the children helped a lot. Instead of being horrified when all his hair had gone, they called him Uncle Kojak."

Bob's own sense of fun wasn't completely lost, either. He bought four wigs in different colours to help him if he "got into trouble," as he describes the seemingly endless romances which he conducts in the same unflamboyant but deceptively rapid way in which he rides.

Yet through all those long bad days, one almost ridiculously stubborn streak stood out—Bob's obsessive wish to ride again. Ironically, it nearly prevented him from taking the treatment at all. "When I first explained that it would take six months," says the specialist, "he said, 'In my business I will be forgotten in six months. I would rather take my chance, and last as long as possible.'" Fortunately, when the odds were spelt out and when his trainer, Josh Gifford, stated typically that the job as first jockey was there whenever he returned, the stubborn streak pushed Bob through the treatment even when sometimes it seemed the only thing left.

After he had done his riding stint at Saratoga two weeks ago, we took a speedboat on Lake George, that historic 35-mile-long waterway at whose head so many Redskin, Redcoat and Rebel battles were fought. Just one long diagonal scar across his chest was the only trace of the personal battle Bob Champion had been through. There were young ladies beside him, success again up ahead. In what must remain the happiest understatement of this or any other season, he said gently: "Not too bad, is it?"

Just how Bob Champion crowned his comeback with that fairytale win on Aldaniti in the Grand National has long gone into books, film and legend. Time to think for a moment of the almost equally astonishing story that his victory prevented. Fifty-four-year-old John Thorne and his home-bred Spartan Missile who finished second to Bob that extraordinary day in 1981. Here's John getting ready for the fight. The last paragraph of this story has an unwanted and unwitting sequel to it. John Thorne was killed in a racing fall from a young horse in March 1982. But he left us some memories all right.

Thinking Thin with John Bull
February 1981

Those who think that John Bull has long fled these softly softly islands should have been at Shuckburgh in the heart of Warwickshire last Wednesday. They would have found him alive and well in the sturdy, pink-coated and seemingly indomitable frame of hunt master John Thorne.

Mind you, that is something of a slur on Mr Thorne. For while John's presence in front of the Warwickshire Fox Hounds looks a perfect picture of Olde England, the original 18th-century John Bull would have had the vapours if he had been landed with Thorne's schedule over the next three months. It involves Thorne, at the age of 54, entering his 32nd race-riding season with his eyes firmly set on both the Cheltenham Gold Cup and the Grand National.

Old Bull would surely not have recovered if he had known that underneath the deep-cut hunting coat lay not a "full round belly" but a black rubber suit in which John sweats his way through five hours and some thirty heaving, jumping miles three days a week. Like the fox hunt itself, you can talk about John Thorne as an anachronism, but it is better to say it in the warmth of a city office, and not while trying to follow him across country when hounds are beginning to run.

By any normal standards, what John Thorne is trying to do is quite ludicrously absurd, not to say dangerous. For a start, he'll be taking 21 pounds off his heavily-built body, which reaches 13st 7lb every summer, and which has already suffered one serious back injury from racing. But then, in his unflamboyant but stubbornly competitive way, John has never obeyed "normal" standards. His special horse, Spartan Missile, has long proved himself way out of the ordinary, particularly by winning two Foxhunters' chases over the Grand National fences, and the way the two of them have been preparing themselves for the challenges of Cheltenham and Liverpool would make any "professional" trainer choke on his licence form.

Because for all its pretensions, horse racing is only equine athletics, and as in its human equivalent, the leading trainers and coaches tend to insist on the most carefully programmed routines. Not so John Thorne, who bred both Spartan Missile and Polaris Missile, on whom he won Cheltenham's coveted National Hunt Chase in 1966. Where other trainers roll gallops, trim fences and lecture lads, old John climbs on board himself with the glorious, if nerve-testing, attitude that "if they can't take their chance in the hunting field, why should they survive on a racecourse?"

They were taking their chances on Wednesday all right, and whatever you think of vulpicide by dogs rather than by traps, gas or guns, a good galloping day can certainly make your spirits soar. "The unspeakable in pursuit of the uneatable" perhaps, but if you are loaded up on one of John Thorne's horses, and told to follow him, it is also "the speechless after the uncatchable." Never more so than at 1.30 pm after three hours' riding when he spotted the transport box bringing a change of horses.

By the time we reached the box, the ramp was down and John's wife, Wendy, who is to long-suffering what Rip Van Winkle is to sleep, had coffee, port and sandwiches on offer. There was a gulp, a bite, a heave into the saddle and we were off up the road as if John Wayne had just spotted the bad guys making a run for it. There might be quicker horses around than Spartan Missile, but when he sports his great chestnut nine-year-old bulk again at either Haydock or Sandown in three weeks' time, no horse will be stronger. John Thorne thinks it will take at least two races to knock the rust off him, but if he recovers the peak form that has already won nineteen 'chases, a tilt at both of jump racing's two greatest prizes will be no forlorn venture.

Giving up would always be difficult for a man like Thorne, but two things have made it particularly hard for him to do so. One is that crossing the Rhine as an eighteen-year-old member of the Sixth Airborne on 24 March 1945 has made steeplechasing falls seem comparatively innocuous. The other was the tragic death of his son Nigel twelve years ago, which returned John to the saddle just as he was prepared to take a fatherly back seat.

By all ordinary rules, John Thorne is attempting the impossible. You don't have to be a member of his family to feel that if he could stick to Spartan Missile, only the rules would be in danger of being broken.

With Spartan Missile, John Thorne, Bob Champion and Aldaniti, everything seemed possible in that spring of '81, but the most publicized story of all did not have a happy outcome.
Prince Charles had set a considerable part of his heart, time and energy on riding a winner over fences. The target was the Grand Military Gold Cup at Sandown on 14 March, the conveyance a big strong eleven-year-old called Allibar, and for a long time everything seemed well on schedule.

The Prince had a safe but slow ride round Sandown the
previous year on another horse and then he and Allibar ran
a highly creditable second in a big field at Ludlow. More
training through the winter and then, on the walk back
home three weeks before the Gold Cup, Allibar suddenly
staggered, keeled over and died, his heart taken by some
massive burst inside.
In retrospect the enterprise was probably doomed from that
moment because although the substitute horse, Good
Prospect, was talented enough, he didn't have much of a
front on him for an inexperienced rider to balance behind.
It was also the time of the Lady Diana romance and so we
media folk were having a whole county of field days. Yet
the Prince pushed on, got to Sandown fit and trim and was
actually making significant ground on the leaders when
Good Prospect clouted the fifth fence from home and his
rider stepped unhappily out the front door.

Princely Imperative: should have done well
March 15th 1981

His Royal Highness's Good Prospect slipped, the Prince of Wales went overboard and the royal claret flowed. Some thought it a joke, some an unacceptable
risk of State. It was neither. It was a very good day for sport.

For the fascinating thing about Prince Charles's mishap (and minor nosebleed)
at Sandown's eighteenth fence on Friday was his attitude to what, let's not dodge
it, is the humiliation every rider dreads. One slight misjudgement and you are
dumped on the grass, while the horse, and the whole time-capsule of the race,
spin irretrievably on.

But after undergoing the most public return to scale of any unseated rider, and
the usual papparazzi ordeal when he later walked to the stables, he was neither
despondent nor self-deceiving. "It was such a pity," he said. "I felt we were just
getting into the race, but he just needs a bit more organising, and there is so little
time. If people could understand."

There were the usual assorted bigwigs taking tea in Sandown's holy of holies,
but only one who had ridden that afternoon. And it showed. "I was so thrilled to
be out there and doing it at last," said the Prince, carving lumps out of the Stilton
as only a wasted jockey can. And even if it came to nothing, you have got to learn
from setbacks. I am pleased I got myself so fit. I am sure that this helps you in a
fall."

When he talks like that, the voice is warmer and softer than you expect. You
also notice that the lean, lined cheeks have something of an outdoor ruddiness

you don't associate with public men. For all the Prince's head-tilted politeness, there is an almost evangelical fervour when he talks about fitness ("I couldn't do my job if I wasn't fit"). And also about the mental discipline of taking up challenges, and conquering fear.

"You see, I had lost my nerve for riding when I was about fourteen," he said after walking the squelchy Sandown track that morning. "So my ambition was to go hunting. My sister is such a good judge that she bought me the perfect horse about five years ago, and I got my confidence back. I wish people could realise what a wonderful all-round riding school hunting is. And then I started doing those team chases, and after that this seemed a logical progression."

Logical it might be, and for the ordinary, fit, successful young executive, not that difficult to organise, provided your weight isn't too bad, you can ride frequently in a racing stable and get plenty of practice on the racecourse. But for the 32-year-old managing director of Great Britain Ltd, with an international diary committed six months in advance, with upwards of half a stone to lose off a normally fit body-weight and with little chance of sustained riding out, let alone racing experience, the task of making yourself competent in one of the most demanding and specialised sports would seem impossible.

Trainer Nick Gaselee chose his words carefully on Friday morning. "It has," he said, "been a remarkable performance. I suppose Prince Charles started arriving in November 1979, and last winter might have averaged two mornings a week. This time it's only been three times a fortnight. He has only had three race rides, yet he has improved all the time. Obviously I have tried to point things out, we have twice used a videotape of the gallops and I gave him John Hislop's book (the definitive text book of steeplechasing). Of course, losing Allibar three weeks ago has been a terrible blow, as they really knew each other, but the Prince is very, very fit."

The man himself shows obvious delight in having got into condition. "My weight is a problem, but I just tell people I can't eat too much because of the riding, and today I'm just under eleven stone. I have done the Hislop exercises religiously (imitation jockey crouches) and I'm very keen on bicycling. For instance, on Wednesday I managed to get down to Windsor for an hour, and bicycled round the park for forty minutes out of the saddle."

Indeed, the Prince's bicycle was the one thing that *was* on that famous Duchy of Cornwall train, and "the achiever" in him likes to relate how he did eleven miles round the steep country lanes in fifty minutes. Just as on his shatteringly intensive skiing holiday, he did the Weissfluhjoch-Kublis Run in just fourteen minutes before finishing second in the all-day Parsenn Marathon.

Nevertheless, steeplechasing is a risky business, so what do his advisers and the future Princess, sitting patient and lovely at the end of the table, think of these sporting plans? There is a sigh at the familiar question. "Well I try to be as sensible as possible. Not ride novices, cut down the risks. But if people could just understand the real thrill, the challenge of steeplechasing. It's part of the great

British way of life, and none of the other sports I've done bears any comparison."

Timid royalists can take comfort that the Prince is still twelve rides short of even being qualified to race in the Grand National. "And at this rate," he said, "it will take six years!" Besides the outside chance of riding in the Kim Muir Memorial Chase at Cheltenham on Tuesday, his next possible ride is on 26 May.

But if people think that in steeplechasing he is just going to be a three-rides wonder, they should have seen his mischievous grin when he said: "You see, I have this awful thing of wanting to do things well." The one bet you can have is that this Prince will return.

Well, it wasn't much of a bet, because although he did return he was a three, or in fact four, rides wonder. Prince Charles rode Good Prospect the next Tuesday at Cheltenham, but the old horse who had unseated ace amateur Jim Wilson earlier in the season didn't have any great difficulty in severing his royal connection for the second time in a week. The Prince had one more ride, unplaced at Newton Abbot, but since then such minor matters as the royal wedding, global tours, and Great Britain Limited seemed to have ruled out the chance of an ambition which, granted the right beast beneath him, was well within his compass.
Three months after Sandown, and seven weeks before all the shenanigans at St Pauls, another, slightly younger although rather more experienced rider was getting almost royal headlines. His name was Walter Swinburn.

Swinburn's Date with Destiny
May 24th 1983

The Rockwell College scrum-half looked so tiny when he ran on to Cork's Musgrave Park for the 1977 Munster Schools' Cup final that many of the twenty thousand crowd just hooted at his titchiness. They didn't laugh once he started to play, and they won't laugh on Wednesday week when, at nineteen, he becomes the youngest jockey in living memory to ride a Derby favourite.

In one sense, Walter Swinburn's journey to the coveted spot on Shergar's back at Epsom has been as smooth as the down on his still almost-unshaven chin. But those who think that the progress from being son of Irish champion jockey, Wally Swinburn, apprentice to the greatest modern-day racing Svengali, "Frenchie" Nicholson, and now first jockey to Shergar's trainer, Michael Stoute, has been an easy climb, should think back to the qualities shown that day in 1977 when the future jockey trotted out to do battle against Presentation College.

At that stage Walter (not Wally to avoid a family "clash") was some thirty pounds lighter and six inches shorter than his present whipcord eight stone and 5ft 6in, and must have looked more like a mascot than a midfield dynamo. "But if the crowd and the other team laughed at him, we didn't," says Rockwell's president, Father Patrick Holohan. "We knew that it had been his dropped goal that had got us to the final, and if we eventually lost 4–3 that day, it was no fault of Walter's, because he was as quick and cool as ever, and showed he could take any amount of punishment."

More predictably than that rugby prowess, or even than the considerable ability shown at soccer, Gaelic football, and cricket, W. Swinburn's name was also inscribed on the show-jumping trophy at the school gymkhana; and the combination of games-winning flair, natural affinity with horses and famous racing connections, made this last recruit just about the likeliest of all the angel-faced little hopefuls who had beaten a path to Nicholson's door ever since he took Paul Cook to the apprentices' championship back in 1964.

Since "Frenchie" also knocked me into shape good enough to ride a hundred winners, you can imagine that he was something special as a teacher. A ludicrously hard worker himself (he had usually mucked out about four boxes before 7 am), his motto used to be, "It's the little things that count." And morning after morning, as the string scrambled its way up Cleeve Hill, above Cheltenham, like a mountain mule-train, he used to coax, bully, instruct, and above all, boyishly share with you the basics of the jockey's craft.

To these, young Walter was strange, having ridden only hunting and show-jumping before. "I kept getting run away with by those big jumpers," he remembers with laughter in those large hazel eyes, "and I had to carry my whip, saddle, and even my pitchfork, in my left hand to make me as good one side as the other." Not surprisingly, he proved an apt pupil and in his first season, 1978 ("I would have been happy with twelve rides"), he rode twelve winners.

The comparison with (and if you look today, the modelling on) Pat Eddery is obvious. Himself the son of an Irish champion, Eddery had graduated from Nicholson's care to win four jockeys' championships, and with Mrs Nicholson doing her usual tireless job with arrangements, Swinburn took off in 1979 to all but win the apprentices' title with 47 winners. Yet illness sadly forced "Frenchie" into retirement, Swinburn's indentures were transferred to Reg Hollinshead's Staffordshire stable, and you could argue that Walter's progress, with 49 winners last year, was slowing.

Well, maybe the winner-rate was. But the widening of the talent, and the credit in professional circles certainly weren't, and last autumn's famous Eddery–Piggott–Mercer job change-round gave Walter the greatest challenge and, some thought his biggest problem—the chance to be first jockey to Michael Stoute's 110-horsepower string at Newmarket.

The Jeremiahs suggested that the pressure might be too much, and Walter himself said last week that his first ride for the stable was his most nervous of the season. But while Stoute's own deep-voiced support ("I have no doubts about Walter. I have never had any doubts.") and ability to run a happy and remarkably democratic ship have no doubt been contributing factors, the truth is that out on the track Swinburn doesn't look so much like a boy doing a man's job as a young star making senior riders feel their age.

Greville Starkey must have heard the old scythe swishing a bit at Goodwood on Thursday. Having got the last flawless professional ounce out of Quality of Mercy, he was short-headed by Walter Swinburn. As the young hero was led back in triumph, and as he later talked about Shergar's power and mobility, you remembered his father, who may well ride Dance Bid against him at Epsom, speaking of the shock of "realising that he wasn't just a son, but a highly-tuned opponent."

Indeed, the more you study Swinburn, the more you realise that the riding won't be a problem. Maybe the weight (but it looks stabilised at around 8st 3lb), maybe the problems of broadening out from the present dedicated puritanism of youth (no heavy girlfriends, and hardly a drop to drink). That's when you remember something else Father Holohan said about his scrum-half. "He wasn't just a fine little athlete, he was dedicated to doing what was right." If that remains so, Shergar's Derby could be the first of many for Walter Swinburn.

Shergar won all right, a mere twelve lengths, the longest margin in Derby history. Yet for all his precocious talent, Walter was still some way short of the weekly stream of winners that bring a championship. In 1981 it was Willie Carson who was ahead. Until 18 August at York. The filly Silken Knot crashed over, breaking both forelegs—and quite a bit of Carson too.

Pump Back Soon, Willie
August 23rd 1981

By Thursday evening the spare bed in the hospital room was laden down with thirteen bundles of get-well cards, while five bunches of grapes and a whole garden of flowers fought for any space remaining. Willie Carson's public had not forgotten him.

It wasn't much consolation, for two days on from his horrific accident at York's Ebor meeting, the little man looked a mess. Propped up wincingly on a mound of pillows, with blackened eyes, plastered left arm and cuts on top of the nose and behind the ear, he was suddenly like some tiny, battered Dorian Gray. Willie, the Human Dynamo, the Flying Scot, the Cheeky Champion, beloved by punters and headline writers alike, was looking every month of his 38 years, and feeling every yard of the long hard road he slogged to reach the top.

Thinking back to Tuesday afternoon, when the ambulance was creeping up the racecourse with that agonising slowness which usually betokens a fractured skull or broken back for its occupant, and to the dismay with which we waited for the first hospital bulletins, it should have been a joy to have any conversation at all with Carson on Thursday. But after the euphoria caused by the news that, despite fractures to the skull, wrist and vertebrae, there was no long-term damage, this was the grim realisation that someone who has become the symbol of bounce and energy to a wide public would be out of our lives for some time.

He hadn't slept much the night before, and the strain of giving a passable imitation of his usual chirpiness was all too clear. Although he had full recollection of the accident ("The filly broke her leg—I never had a chance, but I even remember being in the ambulance"), there was a weary drowsiness about him that only disappeared with the news that Lester Piggott had won another race on an intended Carson mount. "This is the best thing that has happened to Lester," said Willie. "If I had been around, he would have been a very tired man by the end of the season. Now he can take it easy and coast home in the jockeys' championship."

(With 114 winners, Carson was eleven ahead of Piggott at the time of the accident; by this morning, Lester had cut the lead to three.)

Like his chest, so strangely fleshy for one so supremely fit, the remark was stripped bare, devoid of the chuckling banter that is the usual Carson public delivery. Suddenly you could see through to the raw, to that original primitive determination that made him the toughest, even if the smallest newspaper boy in his native Stirling, that bore him through the slowest start of any champion jockey this century (at age 22 he had only ridden 22 winners), that is still his greatest quality, but which has also cost him dear.

Not just the usual bumps and strains of a top jockey's life—after Willie's first championship he went to bed and slept for three days—but on the personal side, where the observer may find determination and selfishness hard to separate, and where his own marriage, once the spur to his great push upwards, ended in unpleasasnt acrimony. Since then, one long-standing relationship has come and gone, and now the devoted and pinkly pretty Elaine Williams sits at the bedside. This time, one hopes, things can settle happily, yet only with the realisation that what makes him a better jockey has also made the living more difficult.

For while he retains his distinctive, energetic riding style, he has added a lot more cunning to his craft. Where he used to say: "That's me, just keep on pumping," he can now remark privately about a famous rival: "It's easy to beat him—he's so predictable." He has also formed a lasting relationship with that most demanding of all mistresses—the general public. All kinds of people who once thought that jockeys were wordless wonders who other people either slagged or praised, became involved with racing through Carson's infectious good cheer on radio and TV. In that sense he has been, quite simply, the best ambassador the game has ever had.

To those near him, the act has sometimes worn a little thin. That is the classic dilemma of the national hero: it is easier to deal with the adoring public than with those closer home. Maybe, but that's not the thought you took away from York District Hospital. For it had been no act by their most famous patient when he shrugged his shoulder in painful sympathy as he watched a TV programme on Riding for the Disabled. "The strangest people write to me," he said. "One lady said that when she came to see me at Leicester races it was the first time she had been out of the house for three years."

She won't be the only fan who, until next season, will miss her little touch of Carson at the track.

Not surprisingly, Carson took his time a-mending. But he had his title back by the end of '83. He actually returned to race riding at Doncaster in March 1982 and by then had seen three months' living proof that modern science and timeless determination can put almost anything back together. That proof was Jonjo O'Neill.

Jonjo: Healed, Happy, Humble and Heroic
December 1981

No one remembers what Lazarus did afterwards, but from the look of Jonjo O'Neill at Newcastle yesterday, he is set on making a lot more of his comeback than just the act itself.

One winner from five rides around the muddy, testing ground of Gosforth Park brought his total to four winners from 21 mounts since he returned from his fourteen-month lay-off to ride a winner at Wetherby on Tuesday. And yesterday, as he unzipped his boot and removed the padding from the right leg he horrifically damaged last autumn, Jonjo looked boyishly around the familiar backcloth of saddles, girths, towels and sweat and said happily: "Honestly, I don't give the leg a thought now."

But the present success of the venture should never cloak the enormity of the problem O'Neill faced when he could fully focus through the screaming pain at Bangor-on-Dee 412 days ago. In a freak mid-air accident after he had been thrown clear from his falling horse, his shin had been snapped in 36 pieces by the scissors motion of another horse's flailing hind legs. Not only was his right leg reduced "to a bag of gravel," but it was the same limb which had been so badly broken at Stockton five years earlier that the bones stuck out through the leather boot.

Yet the miracles of modern surgery, and the healing qualities of a super-fit 28-year-old were such that he was back within the month to the little stone farmhouse he had just bought in Cumbria, near Penrith, and if prudence had

Jonjo O'Neill back in action, December 1981. A spirit falls couldn't break (Chris Smith)

then run a better second to enthusiasm, last week's return would have happened much sooner. As it was, his premature efforts at full activity shifted the metal plate in his leg, and brought such other pain and complications that by the end of April his devoted surgeons in Carlisle had to recommend sending Jonjo for a last-chance operation at Professor Martin Allgower's renowned surgery in Basle.

There the plate was replaced and strengthened, while a piece of hip-bone was grafted on to the damaged shin, yet there were moments afterwards when Jonjo was low enough to contemplate taking your cautious correspondent's advice that two jockey's championships and a world-record 149 jumping wins in a season were enough for any career. But this time the healing process was good, and some weeks before his fairytale comeback on Tuesday (it even made the children's news), there was plenty of evidence that the man was back in shape.

Yet you have to suspect scars on the mind, as well as on the shin-bone, and since some observers thought they saw something less than the old gale-force O'Neill on Tuesday, we trekked off to the windy, unsung delights of Ayr races on

Thursday to see for ourselves. Jonjo had five rides and no winners, but all were placed, all of them went to the last with a chance, and if their rider lacked commitment, the Himalayas must be flat.

Seeing O'Neill the jockey up close once again makes you marvel at the contrast with the man. Out of the saddle he has a gentle, boyish, countryboy Irish charm; in it, he is a little crouched-up tiger with the most compulsive winner-rate in the game, and as he used arms, whip and banshee yells to persuade Run and Skip to do rather more than that at the final flight, there was no doubt the tiger was back.

As he towelled off his sturdy 5ft 6in, 9st 5lb frame afterwards, the first impression was of the astonishing level of fitness already reached. The hard-pulling Run and Skip had been his fifth ride in succession—a total of thirteen miles and 67 obstacles at racing pace—yet there was no heaving of the chest, nor even a moistening of the brow.

"Ah, yes, I'm fit as a flea," said Jonjo. And then, with that directness which reminds you that the grocer's son from Castletownroche, County Cork, didn't get all this way on easy-going charm, he said: "But I have really grafted, been bicycling all over the Lake District and on the farm I have worked like a slave."

The second impression is that the lay-off, with its other involvements, the farm, his *Daily Mirror* column, milk commercials and numerous store openings, has given him a broader perspective. "I love this game," he said, patting his gingery side-whiskers. "I've always said I would do it for nothing, and that's still true. But after the break I am fresher, hungrier, and with the bank manager after me, I've got to get going." And then, with a quiet wisdom which other richer sportsmen might ponder, he added: "I may not have learnt much more about racing in the past year, but I certainly have about people."

Talking to him last Thursday, just a couple of miles from the birthplace of Robert Burns, there was nothing fanciful in recalling the famous lines: "Gie fools their silks and knaves their wine, a man's a man for a' that." Sporting triumph this may be, but the most important memory of the week is of the remarkable, humble, happy man that is Jonjo O'Neill.

Jonjo got back but obviously it was far too late to play any part in the jockeys' championship. That season a beautifully contrasting battle was developing at the head of affairs. We called it . . .

Duel of 1982: Hunger against Art
January 3rd 1982

Beware superlatives, but as we turn into '82 there is the immediate prospect of one of the classic duels of this or any other year. A uniquely gifted champion tested by a supremely motivated challenger for the hardest-won prize in sport.

John Francome against Peter Scudamore for the jump jockeys' title.

This morning, half way through the ten-month season, Francome has a handy lead but, injuries permitting in the 400-odd races which separate each jockey from the dog-days of July, we are promised a battle which contrasts everything from riding styles to the personalities of the men themselves. Francome, 29 years old and three times champion, superbly relaxed both in and out of the saddle; Scudamore, 23, with only three full seasons behind him and so intense that one admiring fellow professional said last week: "He's got to change, or he will kill himself."

The picture taken at Newbury last November, says plenty on what both jockeys are about. Francome is riding Major Swallow for his retaining Fred Winter stable, and even at this downward parabola of the leap, he is as forward-poised as in any picture from his show-jumping youth. Scudamore is on the more fancied Leney Duel from the David Nicholson stable. He has had to gamble on a more extravagant jump, and now has to give his horse every inch of rein to stretch his neck on landing. Then he will flash that right hand down the rein in the orthodox jockey's ways, and shorten up his hold as the horse comes away from the fence.

It's Francome style that's original, and he has in fact two match-winning qualities—his perfect balance and placing of a horse's jumping stride, and his saucy "cool" and timing through a race. Both attributes are so much a gift that they evoke Louis Armstrong's famous answer to the woman who asked for his definition of rhythm: "Lady, if you gotta ask, you ain't got it."

But it's worth explaining that if ordinary jockeys adopt as forward a position as Francome throughout a steeplechase jump, they end up going "out the front door" if the horse hits the fence or slips on landing. And although it's easy to write about the need to keep a cool head in a race, in practice the craving to strike heedlessly for home is so strong that many more races are lost by a finishing effort made too early than too late.

John is not much more forthcoming about how he does it but he does say: "I have got very long legs and arms, so staying close to a horse isn't very difficult." More seriously he adds, "It may be something to do with the eyes. I have got very good eyesight, and making horses jump has never been a problem. As to keeping calm, I am just lucky I'm not the worrying type."

However it's done, the plain facts need stating that Francome's methods win countless races lesser mortals have lost through faulty jumping, and his extraordinary coolness takes as many more from those who play their aces too early.

But such credentials should never cloud the fact that Peter Scudamore too has some impressive cards to put on the table. With 91 winners last year, he has made a meteoric rise in the history of the game, and if he hadn't cracked his skull last April he might be champion already. Son of Michael Scudamore, who won the Grand National on Oxo, and retained by David Nicholson, he has had the finest grounding in the professional game, as well as an A-level public school educa-

Two champions in one picture. Peter Scudamore (right) and John Francome at Newbury in November 1981 (Chris Smith)

tion. But what sets Peter apart is not the coaching, but a commitment almost frightening in its intensity.

You see this in his serious demeanour, in his lean, honed 5ft 9in figure, at ten stone some ten pounds lighter than the similarly built Francome. But above all, you see it in his riding, which at its best has a compulsion which has even hardened racegoers whistling through their teeth. Apparent no-hopers find themselves not discreetly hacking around the back, but crammed up into the favourite's berth, and such confidence has been repaid frequently enough for Scudamore to have become a punter's idol.

The criticisms have been that as a man he has seemed too single-minded, and that as a rider he is too forceful for his own and the horses' good. The bad news for Francome fans is that neither of these criticism seem as viable as they might have been a year ago. "I may have been a bit tough on horses sometimes," says Peter. "Yet it was only through trying too hard. I never meant to hurt them. When the gate goes up now, I am just as determined, but I am riding better because I am using my brain more, and understand the game a lot better.

He fields the questions in his steady, lucid way: "As to being serious, I am serious because I want to be taken seriously. I don't suppose John Francome made much noise when he had only been around for a couple of seasons. Anyway, with my father in the game, I have seen a lot of big mouths come and go. But I always wanted to be champion jockey from the youngest age, and although I like and admire John a lot, I have to believe I can do it."

Some professionals believe that whatever lead Francome may now build up, the driving hunger of the younger man will overtake him in the closing months of the season. But others have detected a new edge in Francome himself, particularly in a finish; that the man with all the gifts, whose renowned coolness in the saddle could sometimes lapse into casualness, has sharpened up his act.

So let's bring forward a surprise witness. J. Francome, jockey, housebuilder, tennis nut, fish-and-chip mogul, wit and (on Saturdays) bon viveur. "All this stuff about me not caring has begun to get up my nose," says the man who for years has revelled in the claim that his only motives are mercenary. "Peter's challenge has probably done me good, but besides taking the overall title three times, I've been the leading jockey in the South for the past seven years, and I want it to stay that way."

Sounds like a champion stung. Seems like a space to watch.

Successful tips don't always flow from this quarter so it's nice to say that six months after that article was written, Francome and Scudamore dead-heated for the National Hunt jockeys' championship, albeit courtesy of Francome who would not pass the 120 total (and twenty-odd lead) amassed by his injured rival.
Two championships for the price of one, perhaps, but in the Autumn of '82 we had another sort of wonder. It was that the combined ages of Francome and Scudamore would only just beat the seniority of a tiny visiting flat-race jockey. He was unique.

A Man who Leaves Piggott Amazed
October 24th 1982

You may be old, Father William, but you still get it right. Bill Shoemaker was back in town from California last week, and with him one of the abiding mysteries in modern sport. How does he do it? How does this tiniest of international stars make racehorses run as if the very hounds of hell were behind them?

You can be sure brute strength and compulsion have little to do with it. Fifty-one years old now, 7 stone with a good lunch inside him and still only 4ft 10in in his size 1½ socks, Willie the Shoe was the oldest, smallest and, in strictly muscular terms, weakest of the eight riders in Sandown's glorious Britain v United States competition on Wednesday. Yet when the jockeys pulled their muddy goggles down at the end of the first race, it was once again Shoemaker who came back to the winner's circle after the 8,183rd victory of the most successful riding career in racing history.

Bill Shoemaker, small only in stature. The world's most successful jockey, with over 8,000 winners, including (left) the 1981 Arlington Million on John Henry (above: Chris Smith; below: Gerry Cranham)

Three furlongs from home, things hadn't looked so bright. Shoemaker had been behind everything bar the reluctant Dudley Wood, with the long Sandown hill in front of him. Worse, when he tried to challenge on the near rails, the passage was as blocked as Piccadilly in rush hour. Then it happened. Shoemaker didn't just switch position, he altered course about 45 degrees to starboard, and with the momentum of a dinghy bearing away from the wind, he and the filly Aura swept right round the pack to challenge on the far side. There was no Piggott coiled-spring and then whip-cracking compulsion, no Carson pumping insistence, but just this miniature jockey crouched so low in Aura's mane that, excepting some upright flourishing of the stick, you could almost think she was galloping loose.

Unbelievers will suggest that as Aura was favourite she might have won anyway. But, apart from the 25–1 and 14–1 starting prices of Shoemaker's two winners at the first Sandown International in 1980, critics miss the uniqueness of the manoeuvre. As with two other Shoemaker successes in Britain (Pelay at Sandown and Rose du Soir at Ascot) it was achieved very much against the rule of the quickest way being the shortest route. The only local comparison I can remember are some of Stan Mellor's challenges under jumping rules, and it is an interesting coincidence that he, too, had a record number of winners.

Mellor was also smaller and lighter than most of his colleagues, but even his appetite for life could not equal that of Mr Shoemaker for, unhindered by weight worries, Bill is quite happy to carouse the night away, and on Wednesday morning it was almost commuter time before the little man took to his bed. "It's quite ridiculous," said his European "minder", Charles Benson, of the *Daily Express*, Ascot and Annabel's (not necessarily in that order). "I'm about three times Bill's size, yet although he doesn't get drunk, he can put me under the table. Then, next morning, he can ride races, play ten-handicap golf and good tennis as if nothing has happened."

Visions of some Lilliputian roisterer don't survive a meeting with Shoemaker himself. Although privately prone to such amusements as placing lifelike rubber snakes and scorpions in colleagues' hotel rooms, Bill's public persona is almost majestic in its quiet dignity and entire lack of conceit. "I just love coming to England and riding English horses," he said, dressed in immaculately tailored grey slacks and check tweed jacket, and with his leggy and lovely wife, Cindy, as ever by his side. "Your racing is very different, the pace is slower but I guess a horse is still a horse."

His third marriage has brought the added happiness of Bill's first child, Amanda, born in 1980, and there is no doubt that this golden evening of his career is his happiest stretch yet. But what of the magic that has brought record winnings of over ninety million dollars to this best and smallest of Texas exports?

"Well, I never had any racing background," he recalled, with those thin lips hard against the teeth as if pressed there by the wind of his 35,000 rides on the track. "Just a teacher suggested I be a jockey because of my size, and it seemed to work. I rode 219 winners straight off in my first season up in California. I am not a great whip rider, or a special hard rider, but just seem to make them run."

For Americans, discussion of Shoemaker's evergreen genius became old hat long ago. His association with a whole host of racehorses, and most recently with Spectacular Bid and John Henry, has left them echoing the easy statement, "He makes them run." But Steve Cauthen, one of his team mates on Wednesday, is more specific: "Bill doesn't do a lot, but he keeps beautifully in the centre of balance, so that a horse can run for him more easily, and he's always prepared to wait until he thinks they are ready." And with the confidence born of his first hundred-winner season in Britain, Cauthen added, "Horses respond to a rider's feel, and Bill can sense a horse and make them believe in themselves."

Maybe that explains it, but not for everyone. Not even for the one jockey whose legend (if not his winners in GB v USA matches) matches Shoemaker's own. "He's a phenomenon," said Lester Piggott, pondering hard on the rider he respects most in the world. "Some of the things he does, with his whip and his reins in a tangle, you would think would slow horses down, but they just go faster." Then the famous muttered tones took on an almost far-away sound as he continued: "That filly Aura on Wednesday was turning it in a furlong out. She had her head on one side. Wasn't going to win . . . then she did . . . it was an extraordinary thing. Something you cannot explain."

You may be old, Father William, but sometimes you have the laugh on us yet.

Piggott may have been dishing out compliments in Shoemaker's case but at the time he was also very much on the receiving end. It had been one of his very best seasons. It seemed time to take tea.

Lester's Rich and Very Mellow Autumn
October 31st 1982

Another year over and deeper in his debt. Love him or hate him, Lester Piggott has once again cast the longest shadow over the flat racing season which ends this week. What's more, with 188 winners so far, he's even managed a smile or two. As a matter of fact, he smiles quite a bit, the sunshine warming the wintry landscape of his face, and as he finishes this, his 35th riding season, it's time to revise the accepted image of Britain's longest-serving star.

Piggott may still be bleak and taciturn in public, his perception of wage rates may still be the envy of any union leader, and with a seven-day 1,200-mile week from March to November, he may still be on the most relentless treadmill in sport. But a couple of hours with him on Friday evening left an overriding impression of a man almost blissfully happy in his work.

"Of course I enjoy it all. There wouldn't be any point in doing it otherwise," he said, the sentences as lean and spare as the limbs beneath the fawn slacks and

Lester Piggott, genius in the saddle (Chris Smith)

grey check sweater. "I still get a kick out of every ride, every winner. All horses, every race is different. The challenge is to get them right."

Lester was talking in the long, low living room of his ranch-style house on the edge of Newmarket. On the table the telephone, the big blue diary and the form book were reminders of the obsessive planning behind the triumphs recorded on the walls around him. As usual, a big cigar was the only nourishment, but those famous nasal tones were soft, at times almost purring, like the black cat beside him on the sofa. So benign a Piggott is a surprise. We are used to him in the eye of the storm, the body angled high above the saddle, the face lined and sinister beneath the goggles, that we forget the obvious—that, for all his ever-hungry drive, Lester probably has more reason to feel satisfied than anyone in Britain.

He's 47 on Guy Fawkes Day, and yet needs only four more winners this week to pass his best-ever season's total of 191 successes, even if the much-coveted two hundred-mark is now out of reach. What's more, he's done it with far more economy of effort. "It's much easier now I am riding for Henry Cecil rather than Vincent O'Brien. It's got to be. All the horses are here, the plans are here, not

Photo: Chris Smith

three hundred miles away in Tipperary. I couldn't manage that any more. Henry's given me five more years, really."

The teaming with Cecil has obviously been the central ingredient. But this final flourish that has brought Piggott his tenth and eleventh championships has also depended on two other factors, his continued fitness and judgement. "I've been very lucky this year. Hardly a fall," he says, and while he pauses to relight the cigar, you remember the ear-tearing crash at Epsom which has necessitated the special helmet ear-cover. If he's pressed as to nerve and judgement, there is one of those shrugs and opening of the hands, but the answer is precise. "Provided you enjoy it, it gets easier as you get older. It's experience. It all gets slower. You think quicker, see the problems earlier, so you have more time."

Which brings us to the "When will you hang up your boots?" question. It's an old chestnut, and is given an old reply: "Dunno. Two or three years I suppose," that has been current for at least a decade. But does he really want to go training, get involved in all the hassle of a trainer's lot he has so painfully described? How long would he need to get readjusted? Future rivals should beware the readiness as well as the chuckle as Lester echoes an old TV answer: "About five minutes."

When he goes, the weighing room will lose the most vivid, consuming talent in its history. It will also miss the master of the Brando-esque one-liner. In Chicago, for the Budweiser Million this August, I ended up doing Sheikh Mohammed's owner's duties for Piggott's horse, Noalto. I bottled it. Instead of giving my jockey a serious lecture on tactics, I lamely asked: "What's your plan, Lester?" That long look and then the muttered reply: "See those starting stalls. Then one-and-a-half circuits." I don't know what Noalto thought, but Piggott nearly died laughing.

Piggott may be a 24-carat phenomenon, but he's really almost normal compared to the lady who came over to win the Champion Hurdle in 1984. To be truthful, she didn't actually ride the winner herself. But she did just about everything else.

A Dawn Run with the Banned Granny
March 4th 1984

Sometimes in Ireland you are sure the leprechauns are laughing at you. Here was their champion racehorse thundering round a Kilkenny field on Wednesday morning with, astride it, not some thick-shouldered jockey-boy, but a little old lady so small and frail-looking that you want to keep the grandchildren off her at teatime.

Dawn Run is the horse, whose twelve brilliant victories make her the spearhead of this month's annual Irish invasion of the Cheltenham Festival. Charmian Hill is the rider, at 65 some 59 years senior to her mare, and with an approach to racehorse ownership about as far from the modern trend of "quadruped as commodity counter" as trainer Paddy Mullins's easy-going country yard in Munster is from Aqueduct, New York.

Not for Mrs Hill the vague weekly phone-call or the distant view of the nag on the gallops. She not only bought Dawn Run herself and completed the then three-year-old filly's early education, she was also in the saddle on a golden day in the summer of '82 when Dawn Run sped away from a big field at Tralee for the first success of what has been one of the most meteoric climbs in Irish jumps.

Sadly it was also Charmian Hill's final race-ride, for that very morning she had received a letter from the Irish racing authorities telling her she would be licenced no longer. "I think it was very unfair because I was riding better than ever," says this extraordinary little grandmother of nine without a trace of humour. "So I said to myself, 'Wow—this is one race we are going to win.'"

More cautious souls might have thought it something of a wonder that Mrs Hill had a licence at all after surviving the terrible crash which had killed her horse

Charmian Hill rides Dawn Run in preparation for the 1984 Champion Hurdle (Chris Smith)

Yes Man at Thurles two seasons earlier. Three months in hospital with crushed ribs and vertebrae, and with pins to keep her head atop the neck, took thirty pounds off the old lady's already bird-like eight stone, and for ordinary mortals would have left an afternoon's knitting as the height of achievement.

But even her family have long since stopped trying to fit the year's most unlikely sportsperson into any cosy mould. "Ah, we let her do her own thing," says her husband, Eddie, whose patients in Waterford were no doubt intrigued when the doctor's wife took to point-to-pointing at the ripe old age of 41, and then amazed as she continued to defy the years, moving on to bigger things when Irish racing allowed women to ride against men in 1973, finally bringing off a remarkable treble, winning on the flat, over hurdles and over fences (at the first attempt), all on the ill-fated Yes Man.

Write this down enough times, and the fact that granny's galloping is now confined to hunting and early-morning training spins seems almost mundane stuff. Well, it didn't look too dull when Dawn Run was led out of the box last Wednesday morning. After all, this rangy, hard-faced mare is on the crest of the wave, making her a real threat to the Champion Hurdler, Gaye Brief, whom she had already beaten at Kempton. She's also no respector of persons, being as good at striking out with her front legs as kicking with the back, and having a ruthless style of galloping best summed up by the legendary Irish orders: "Jump off in front and keep improving your position."

Such horses are usually treated with a degree of awe in keeping with the weight of money Dawn Run will carry when Jonjo O'Neill heads her towards the first hurdle on Tuesday week. But Paddy Mullins hasn't saddled a thousand winners in such varied spots as Newmarket, Fairyhouse and Auteuil without developing the knack of turning special circumstances to his advantage. Now, as his wife and sons watched Mrs Hill gathering speed on consecutive laps of the large grass field outside the barn, he simply nodded with the wise satisfaction of a man who never uses ten words when one will do, and said: "The mare enjoys herself."

When the Cheltenham battle honours are settled at the end of next week, with the usual lion's share for the Irish, many of us will shake our heads and wonder how they do it. If Dawn Run can draw Gaye Brief's trumps in the Champion Hurdle, some may even remember that Dr Hill's talents stretch to such things as sawing people in half at charity parties. "I've never done it to Charmian, but I have pulled her out of a few tablecloths," he said. "And I once got three people fainting in the front row when I sawed a boy's head off in Killarney."

The Irish don't need magic to win at Cheltenham—they've got enough of it already.

Photo: Chris Smith

The day after this was written, Gaye Brief went lame and so Dawn Run was clear to collect at Cheltenham and the astonishing Mrs Hill was chaired aloft like some elderly song-bird—and Dawn Run went on to complete a unique Champion Hurdle treble in France in Summer 1984. In April that year another fairly unusual act of triumph was seen in the Cheltenham winner's enclosure. The National Hunt Jockeys' World Championship was upon us and our first winner was celebrating oriental style.

The Yen to be Number One
April 15th 1984

Maybe they did laugh at Columbus in 1492. But then we all hooted at Shinobu Hoshino only last Thursday. Fulke Walwyn, the royal trainer, didn't. He jabbed a forefinger at the hapless Japanese and growled: "Number one. Understand? This is going to win. Number one." At this mounting-up stage in the Cheltenham paddock, many people were thinking that the magnificently ambitious National Hunt jockeys' world championship, its Railfreight sponsorship notwithstanding, was rapidly shunting itself into some Gloucestershire Gilbert and Sullivan opera with a neigh in every line.

We had already endured a whole series of press conferences, culminating in an astonishing marquee lunch where a white-jacketed, red bow-tied harmony group introduced the twelve champions with a number set to the tune of "The Twelve Days of Christmas" ("and so to you . . . we say, *Bienvenus*"). But now we were at the crunch with the assorted heroes leading their interpreters towards some of the most bemused trainers in the history of the game.

For while it had been a grand idea of Bob Champion's to gather the world's top jump riders together for a four-race series, and a truly fantastic achievement actually to land them at Cheltenham on schedule (by plane, not goods wagon), the whole thing becomes just another publicity stunt unless the professionals at the centre can take it seriously.

Fulke Walwyn may be 73, but he's still the sort of competitor who gets upset when his stable lads' second darts team are beaten in a play-off. He was running Desert Hero in the first race. Shinobu Hoshino was to ride it and, despite the 33-year-old jockey's multiple victories in such tongue-twisters as the 65 million Yen Tokyo Shoga Tokubetsu, Walwyn wasn't happy with what he saw.

Even if Shinobu, with his shiny white goggles and dapper black-and-red-plastic boots, was a model of smiling, bowing politeness, he was several sizes smaller than the jump jockey, British version. In fact, he only just pulled eight stone in full kit; so Desert Hero's allotted weight of 11st 11lb had to be made up with lead enough to roof St Paul's. There was also a rumour that the little knight from

Shinobu Hoshino wins at Cheltenham in April 1984 (Chris Smith)

Nippon had changed colour the moment he saw the huge undulations of the Cheltenham track.

All around Fulke and "Shino" other trainers were greeting their new pilots with equal, if not quite such uncomprehending, scepticism. All, that is, except Fred Winter who, by a piece of almost unfortunate good fortune, had drawn his own stable ace, John Francome, out of the hat. Among the others, Josh Gifford faced the neat, if slightly boyish-looking, German, Andreas Wöhler; David Nicholson gave several volumes of instruction to the Norwegian Morten Reinert; Richard Hickman had the ice hockey-playing American Ricky Hendriks, and Derek Gillard had come up from Barnstaple to be given the raffish-faced Italian, Gianantonio Colleo.

Waiting to ride in later races were the moustachioed Belgian, Philippe Caus, the brilliant but battered-lipped Frenchman, Michel Chirol, and the self-possessed young Russian, Husei Kasaev. Chirol had the dubious distinction of being old enough to have actually ridden round Auteuil with me, but poor Husei and his team mates, Mahmut and Nikolai, had the more immediate problem of having your correspondent as guide on the early-morning walk of the course.

Minders Mahmut and Nikolai may have been, but they turned out to also be jockeys in their own right, and far from short of humour. As I banged on about the height and difficulty of the open ditch, Mahmut smiled and explained through the long-suffering Geoffrey (Russian from Cheltenham evening classes, not GCHQ) that back home this was called the "English fence", and their biggest obstacles were twice as high and wide. They didn't even complain when poor Husei was pitched heavily off at the last fence in the steeplechase.

So to action. The mounting bell clanged and the crowd (unhappily sparse at around 4,500) went out to watch John Francome make a fool of the foreigners. It's history now, how little Shino settled Desert Hero just behind the leaders, joined Francome at the second last, got yet another beautiful jump at the final flight and then fairly sprinted home up the run-in.

Hoshino came back to unsaddle, flourishing his whip high above his head, and Fulke Walwyn gave his cunning old tiger grin and said: "I had a few quid on once I saw him take the old horse so sweetly to the start. He looked as if he could do the business." Walwyn got 10–1 and, although Francome duly won the next race to sew up the championship, and the Belgian confounded us all by getting the perilous Greenwood Lad to put in a clear round and win the third, it was already much longer odds against the afternoon turning up anything better than Hoshino's ride.

How could it? As the Japanese came back in triumph, one disgruntled punter proceeded to hurl abuse about everything from Shino's parentage to Pearl Harbour. Each volley was greeted by a smile, a bow, and "Thank you, thank you." Many thought Shino didn't understand, but who says he wasn't remembering one of the best and shortest lines in *The Mikado*: "Life is a joke that has just begun"?

This chapter is called "The Parents" to describe all those who influence events away from the hubbub of the race itself, and out of the main line of the trainer's work. That's why we start with that vital limboland through which every racehorse must go—the box drive to the races. We are back in the dog days of August, '73. There are five to get to Yarmouth. So let's not hang about.

The Bread and Butter Side of it
August 1973

The cast-list around the lathered horse in the winners' enclosure is almost as well-known as that for Mother Goose—smiling jockey, beaming lad, jubilant owner and jovial trainer. But there is always a fifth more anonymous man whom many people don't realise is the lynch-pin of the whole operation—the travelling head lad. Last Wednesday there was no feature race to match the £10,000 of yesterday's William Hill Gold Cup. But with three Flat meetings at Brighton, Pontefract and Yarmouth, it was typical of the busy, bread-and-butter side of the business, and the problems for David Tyers, travelling five horses from Gavin Pritchard-Gordon's Newmarket stable to Yarmouth, are those shared by hundreds of other such men all over the country.

Yarmouth is only two-and-a-quarter hours' horse-box drive from Newmarket, so the horses (in this case two colts and three fillies) can travel up in the morning. Yet by 7.30 am, when only the most fanatical of punters is even aware of the runners, Tyers has loaded up two colts in the first horse-box—whatever may happen in Olympic villages, the sexes here are segregated when possible.

The horses are both two-year-olds: Pey, a bay with a white star led in by Joe Scally, an old Irish lad of the brown suit, trilby hat and cardigan vintage, and Ascendant, a more handsome colt, led up the ramp by Ray Swallow, a more casually dressed twenty-year-old, getting this spare "lead up" because the horse's usual lad, "Pim" Ross, is taking his other charge, Trillium, to Brighton.

"Taffy" Williams, the stable's head lad, will have given both horses a bowl of oats on his morning round at 6.30. A quarter of an hour later the lads would have started to arrive and make ready for the journey. Boxes mucked out, horses groomed, hooves oiled. Then the bandages and knee-boots and travelling sheet put on, although both these last two are taken off once the box gets under way.

Tyers is substituting for the stable's No 1 travelling head lad, Eddie Edwards, but he has worked for this yard since before Gavin Pritchard-Gordon succeeded Harvey Leader two years ago. He checks the runners and is briefed on his rendezvous at the racecourse. Then he has to gather all the day's necessary equipment—grooming kit, smart paddock-sheets, lightweight racing bridles, enough oats for another bowl each on arrival at the track, and, of course, the five separate sets of racing silks for the owners of the day.

Overleaf:
Photo: Gerry
Cranham

Finally the big contract box is on the move. The two horses' heads peer through the little space behind the driver, where the two lads and Tyers are sitting. Pey kicks nervously to start with, but Ascendant looks at us with the self-possession of a horse who has been there and won before.

Time passes quickly as everyone begins to rifle through the racing pages and the box-driver's Geordie chat begins even to humour the two other lads, sullen at having been made to ride out that morning. Once we have crossed the last bit of windmill-spotted Fenland to reach Yarmouth, Tyers is all business again. Supervising the unloading, passing the horses into their boxes in the security area and checking all the equipment. By the time he has finished, the process has to be repeated when the three fillies arrive, so that it is not until 10.30 that the horses are fed and relaxed, and then the men can take an hour off themselves.

Tyers goes for a meal on the seafront with David Guest, who will ride the filly, Starlit Night, in the first race and lead up Frensham in the last.

The two small, chunky men are both in their early thirties, and have been contemporaries since they were apprenticed together at Newmarket. Over the hamburger and chips, and with only a touch of bitterness, they tell of those early days at two bob a week, of the apprentices' strike and of how both of them became disillusioned. Guest had some rides, but Tyers none at all.

He says: "I kept getting promises, but nothing ever happened, so in the end I went to the caravan factory. I did six years there, and the money was good enough for me to get married and buy a house, but once I'd got all that, I wanted to come back into racing."

Guest's career followed an exactly similar pattern, and while they both feel strongly they should rely on a higher basic wage rather than the hope of "copping" from a generous owner, they seem to have plenty of hope for better days. They talk of new head lads' association started by Eddie Edwards, and of the ability of the younger breed of trainers to communicate with them. "Take this guv'nor; if he brings someone into the box, he will introduce you. Some of those old trainers just look at you as if you were not there."

Once back on the course, you can see just how important it is that Tyers and the other travelling head lads are there. The working shirt and slacks are changed for a grey suit and tie, the declarations of the jockeys are checked, and each horse is tacked up and led out three quarters of an hour before its race. Then there are five separate turns through the routine of getting the runner saddled and to the start without disaster.

By the end of the afternoon there has been promise, triumph and a little disappointment. From the head-on position of the lads' stand David Guest is seen to get Starlit Night within a neck of winning the first race. The filly, Harbrook, runs poorly in the next, and Frensham finishes a struggling third in the last. And although Pey runs badly in the feature event of the day, the double effort of getting two runners ready and saddled in the event comes to triumph when Ascendant wins in a photo-finish.

So as owners and trainer are overwhelmed by congratulations in the unsaddling enclosure, there's a little ginger-haired figure in the background with a very special smile of satisfaction. Yet there is still a lot of the day to go—getting both sets of horses cleaned up, rested, then loaded up for the return journey.

It's not until 8.15 that the last horse has been fed and the boxes shut back in the cool of the Newmarket evening. Yet the demands of the daily circus continue, and as the trainer speaks on the telephone to another owner, David Tyers is already checking the colours and equipment for the next day.

You wonder why he would leave the easy hours of the factory for what is still only a £1,500-a-year job. But then you remember the image of that little figure in the winners' enclosure, and the satisfaction that he must get from his part in that amazing pilgrimage of hope that is taking a thoroughbred to the races.

When a horse comes back after winning the Derby, he is led through a sea of top hats and silk dresses to a little island of green. Many imagine that this is the moment and place where even Mick Jagger would get "satisfaction". Maybe. But examine this story after Grundy won in 1975 and wonder whether the pride and the personnel don't stretch a bit further than Epsom.

Grundy as Einstein
June 8th 1975

"You can marry Einstein to an actress," said Grundy's breeder Tim Holland-Martin, "but to develop the perfect brain or the special body you have got to have the right upbringing."

Naturally, he was paying tribute last week to his own staff at the Overbury Stud in Gloucestershire, headed by the tireless Peter Diamond, for their part in the life of the stud's first classic winner. But the compliment to Grundy's human handlers can be extended right through the horse's career to the crowning moment of winning the Derby on Wednesday, and the thought of what might have happened to him in lesser hands can also be applied to the fashioning of Pat Eddery's enormous natural talent into the superb fusion of dash and judgment that swept through in triumph at Epsom.

For, like Eddery, Grundy was something special from the start. He was foaled three years ago this April 3 and by midsummer the studhands at Overbury, set amid Housman's "coloured counties" at the foot of Bredon Hill, soon began to tell Holland-Martin and his uncle Ruby, that Word From Lundy's flaxen-maned colt "could really use himself and liked to be bossman in the paddocks."

It had been seven years before that similar reports had been brought to Jimmy Eddery in Co Dublin that young Patrick, the fifth of his 12 children, was showing effortless promise when apprenticed to Seamus McGrath, near the Curragh. Old Jimmy had, of course, been a top-class Irish rider in his day, being second in the Epsom Derby twenty years ago, and Pat's grandfather and three of his uncles were also jockeys. So there wasn't much difficulty in getting the slender young hopeful established at England's most exclusive riding academy, and soon after his fifteenth birthday Pat Eddery moved to "Frenchie" Nicholson's legendary yard at Cheltenham.

Grundy's path to the "right school" was less predictable, for he had to go up to the yearling sales with three disadvantages. First, his sire, Great Nephew was still unproven; second, his dam, Word From Lundy, had only one previous foal and was herself only a winner through staying power; and third, and worst, Grundy's flashy colour ran directly into the prejudice that flaxen manes and tails are best confined to the circus. What saved him was his "presence". After paying 11,000 guineas on behalf of the Italian owner, Dr Carlo Vittadini, bloodstock agent Keith Freeman told Holland-Martin, "I don't know why I have bought that colt, I am not sure of his sire, I don't like dams who just stay, I hate his colour, yet there is something very exciting about him."

Freeman's highly tuned instinct for the potential galloper meant that Grundy came under the care of the marvellous team that Peter Walwyn has assembled at Seven Barrows, Lambourn, and here the parallel with Eddery becomes more exact.

For, just as Eddery's natural courage and drive were controlled, but not blunted by Nicholson, then brought to full bloom by Walwyn, so Grundy's forcefulness and ability were harnessed to produce the racing machine that sped home in 2min 35.5sec last week.

From all accounts he was no easy ride in his early days, viewing the gallops not so much as places of development than as sites for attempts on the world speed record. It was here that Walwyn was able to call on the skilful hands and cool head of his assistant head lad, Mattie McCormack, who, when with Noel Murless, had ridden such good horses as Mysterious, Welsh Pageant and Lorenzaccio. A less patient man than Walwyn might have merely exploited Grundy's brilliant natural speed, but with Mattie McCormack riding the colt at home, and Pat Eddery applying the same quiet lessons of restraint on the track, Grundy has become a relaxed racing machine who (unlike his father who used to cut out the running) gave himself the chance to stay the one-and-a-half miles of the Derby distance.

"I rode him on a long rein and he just lobbed along for the first mile," said Eddery afterwards. "Everything went just perfect." With his usual modesty, he avoided dwelling on the problems he and the horse had had to solve together this season, for, in all three races before the Derby, Grundy had, through force of circumstances, been in front far longer than would be considered ideal. In both the Greenham Stakes in the mud at Newbury and the 2,000 Guineas, through the strikers at Newmarket, the horse pulled too much for his own good.

But most credit of all must go to Grundy himself, for remember that it was only 17 March, the day before he was to start his serious work, that he was kicked in the face only three inches below his nearside eye. A horse with less of what Walwyn calls "the tiger" in him might have lost some of his edge after the hurried preparation, the defeat in the mud at Newbury and the hard race when second in the Guineas.

Yet, on Derby eve, McCormack paid his trainer an extraordinary and prophetic tribute. "I have never sat on a horse so perfectly tuned," he said, "nor have I sat on one who has given me such a *feel* as he has done."

Grundy's story, however warm in this post-Derby euphoria, was very much a success for the mainstream—be it trainer, jockey or breeder. It is not always so. Witness this tale from '78.

A Humble Champion
August 27th 1978

There was some cheering at Kilsby Quarry as the men on the line listened to the William Hill Sprint Championship at York last Thursday. And with good reason. One of them, Len Hall, had bred the winner.

Let's put that in perspective. At £25,000, the William Hill Sprint is one of the richest races of the year, and when Solinus cruised home under Lester Piggott, the horse was clinching his value at millions of dollars now that he is retiring to stud life in Ireland. He is the massive golden pay-off around which much of racing revolves, and in pursuit of which racing's big shots spend fortunes.

When the big winner is led back in triumph, you will usually find that, as well as the euphoric owner and trainer (in Solinus's case, Danny Schwartz and Vincent O'Brien), the victory party includes the breeder, all togged up in his Sunday best and intent on telling you not only that he knew that this horse would be a champion from the day it was born, but that there is a half-brother coming up to the Sales next week which is an even better looker.

But on Thursday you would have had to go back to Kilsby Quarry, just off the M45 in Northamptonshire, to find Len Hall, Solinus's breeder. In his soft Midlands accent, he did indeed tell you how proud he was as he heard the race on the radio. And, yes, he had always thought that Solinus would be a champion from a tiny foal. His wife will say sadly: "It's always 'if'. To think, with a different turning, we might be millionaires like everyone at York, not just the muckers-outers down here." But Len Hall takes it all philosophically.

But the Len Hall story is more than "little man misses out on big fortune." Its greatest part is that he and his mother Beatrice have now, with forty acres and two mares, bred two undisputed champions by flying in the face of just about every breeding expert in the book. The first champion, Solinus's dam, Cawston's

Pride, was, in 1970, the best filly of her own or practically any other generation. Her sire, Con Brio, was so unfashionable that he cost only 198 guineas at stud. Yet that was 198 guineas more than the cost of Solinus's sire, Comedy Star, who charged 400 guineas for Cawston's Pride's first visit, but was so flattered by her attention that the return trip, in Solinus's year, was free.

Comedy Star was a tough, top class handicapper, but a long way short of most people's idea of a suitable mate for such an outstanding individual as Cawston's Pride. "Yes, lots of people laughed at us," said Len. "But we always like the cheaper stallion, and so long as we liked him as an individual, why change?"

Solinus, naturally, has been the biggest hunch of all, but his full brother, Cawston's Clown, was a Royal Ascot winner two years ago, and last week at York his remaining half-brother, Man of Vision, gave proof of limitless promise by running second in the Acomb Stakes. If Solinus's sire, Comedy Star, was an inspired choice, Man of Vision's, Never Say Die, was more so. For at the time of the meeting Never Say Die was an ageing and none-too-successful sultan, and Cawston's Pride was only the second mare he got in foal that year.

Cawston's Pride was carrying Man of Vision when she was sold by Len Hall to Robert Sangster, and that empire builder's far more extravagant plans for her future matings were dashed when she died of a twisted gut. For a time, it seemed as if there was a blight over the whole deal, because when the bereaved Solinus was sold as a yearling, his purchaser, supposedly from the Middle East, turned out to be a non-payer, if not actually a bus conductor from Finsbury Park. But Robert Sangster later found Frank Sinatra's friend, Danny Schwartz, to take over Solinus, and since he kept a share himself, there were plenty of smiles in York's winner's circle, as well as at Kilsby Quarry.

None of the other big moments at York last week better symbolises the glorious uncertainty of a whole glossed-up multi-million-pound business than the crackling radio in Kilsby Quarry on which Len Hall listened to Solinus, the horse he bred, bow out as champion of Europe. Romance like that is not just good for racing—it is essential to it.

When it comes to "they also serve" in British racing, one of the most admirable groups can be seen standing and waiting in the distance . . . at the starting stalls. It's a perilous enough job in summer. But what happens when winter comes?

The Men who Get their Kicks from a Seat in the Stalls
November 12th 1978

It may be of dubious consolation to those intending immediate death in the York area to know that the bulging biceps of one of the city's hearse drivers have been developed by a spring, summer and autumn of shoving half-ton racehorses into starting stalls.

But with flat racing finally bowing out for the season at Doncaster yesterday, the news of Kenny Gibson's slightly macabre winter activities reminds us that not all members of the family are jetting off to sun-kissed beaches.

Gibson is a member of the eight-man Northern stalls team but, since only the team leader, Peter Hickling, and his deputy, Dennis Cutts, are fully occupied with maintenance during the winter, Gibson and his five colleagues have to find alternative jobs.

Last year a member of another team drove a horse all the way to Moscow, and some have flown horses as far as Australia, but this year's ambitions don't stretch quite as far for the Northern team. Three will be working for trainers and another, "Doc" Halliday, returning to his carpentry business in Malton, with as yet no commissions for Gibson's hearse.

There are four starting-stall teams, Northern, Midland, Southern and the Scottish, which also doubles up for extra meetings in the South. From March until mid-November, they are each responsible for, and work with their own set of three qo-stall units, and in their Land Rovers, trailers and buses are among the unsung heroes without whom the whole circus could not continue.

The first race from starting stalls in Britain was in July 1965. Two yearts later, 29 meetings and all the classic races were started from them, and in 1968 they came under the wing of Racecourse Technical Services, the Levy Board subsidiary which also runs the photo-finish, public address and camera patrol. In the ten years since, stalls have become such an accepted part of the racing scene that it takes something like the horrific accident to the French horse, Easter King, before the St Leger to remind us of the stresses involved in loading and caging half a ton of highly volatile racehorse.

For the record, Easter King's fatal accident, caused by rearing backwards in the stalls, was only the second of its kind in Britain, and while a minority of horses continue to kick, bite, rear and occasionally crawl out the front (there was a case on Friday at Doncaster), injuries are mercifully few. Jocky Wally Wharton was rushed to hospital from Ripon last summer after his leg was trapped against the stall in the ugliest incident yet seen for a rider. Happily, Wharton was back in a fortnight, and it's worth remembering that the worst injuries have all happened to handlers. "This year we have been quite lucky—just a few kicks and bites," says Peter Hickling. "But last year poor Trevor Smith got savaged at Ascot, and was badly smashed up, breaking his pelvis." Against disasters like these Hickling and his colleagues have two pillars of support. The first is the teamwork and understanding of the handlers themselves, and the second is information about difficult horses which is passed to them by assistant starters. Every weekend during the season, Gerry Scott, Bill Rees, Simon Morant and Keith Browne, the country's four assistant starters, pass on to each other news on any horses which have given trouble at the stalls.

"I don't mind the work," says Scott, who spends several hours a week combing entry lists. He won the Grand National on Merryman in 1960, and it as fine a citizen as racing has produced, but he adds: "I wish people would realise how much goes into getting the stalls working properly, and what a great job these lads to. We stretch the rules—three tries at entering the stalls—nearly every day to get horses in, yet it is not often you hear much else than criticism."

Well, let's at least put that right here, and record racing's gratitude to the men behind the stalls. Maybe one day they will receive the financial recognition that will enable them to do what one handler did in Ireland. He actually owned a racehorse, and one memorable day at Leopardstown last summer had the unique distinction of loading his horse up at one end of the race and leading it in as winner at the other.

The danger of easy assumptions is one of the simplest, and often most expensive mistakes in this racing business. That's as true at the top end as it can be shameful at the bottom. Anyway, that's an excuse for trying to make some sense out of that enormous multi-faceted creature which is loosely referred to as "The Sangster Empire." This is October 1980. I don't think it has got any simpler since.

The Emperor with the Chequebook
October 12th 1980

Maybe it was post-Arc torpor. Perhaps it was too much of Robert Sangster's Chablis. But after 279 I gave up the count, for that figure was still less than a third of the way through the most extraordinary noticeboard in the racing world. It is on the far wall of the shining new office on the lower ground floor of Sangster's Isle of Man home. It lists every horse he owns or has shares in. And 279 is merely the number, over six countries and 36 trainers, of his racehorses in training.

The other 400-odd name cards that the ubiquitous, silver-haired Miss Markie can pull precisely out of the board are of the mares, stallions, foals and yearlings that complete the Sangster portfolio, which in five years has developed into the most expensive in the history of the game. If the sun never set over the old British Empire, it now hardly ever completes a circuit without some little man in the green-and-blue Sangster silks flashing across one of the racecourses of the world.

Last Sunday it was Detroit winning the Arc de Triomphe in Paris. Yesterday Gonzales won the Irish St Leger at 7–4 on, and My Paddy Boy was fourth in the Australian Guineas in Melbourne. And on Friday, the new star, Storm Bird, will try to prove himself Europe's top two-year-old by winning the Dewhurst Stakes at Newmarket. So the Sangster syndicate's bandwagon, which has running costs of over £40,000 a week and invests nine million dollars annually, rolls on towards another year in the black.

But scribbling down the figures and sipping wine doesn't answer the question with which you have so fearlessly flown to the three-legged island to confront the 43-year-old former Pools tycoon in his long, white-carpeted lair. We all knew he had pots of cash and masses of horses around the globe. And with The Minstrel's Epsom Derby, and two Arcs from Alleged, he must have something more than beginner's luck. But was this quiet, sturdy, conventionally-dressed, ex-public schoolboy really in charge of the whole operation, or was he just a willing cheque book pushed around by wicked uncle Vincent O'Brien and his powerful son-in-law, John Magnier, in Ireland, and by other assorted heavies around the world?

For if you ever needed evidence that jealousy is racing's besetting sin, you should note down a quarter of the comments bandied around about Sangster and his team.

Because with their associates (Sangster usually has a forty per cent stake) they have formed the richest buying group in the world, they have been accused of monopoly. Because they have sold stallions successfully (four middle lights totalled $10 million in the last two months), they are charged with rigging the market. Because some of their greatest hopes (Try My Best and Monteverdi) have failed to fulfil expectations, they are supposed to be deluding the public. And because their top horses have failed in Britain this year, they are supposed to be skint.

Well, from the look of the unlocked Rolls-Royce (where do you take it if you steal it?) that was waiting at the airport, and the splendour of their former nunnery home, the wolves are still a yard or two away from the front porch. And when you start lobbing the questions at Sangster, he comes back with a directness that makes you remember that for all his dimple-chinned niceness he has already managed a major commercial firm at Vernons Pools, and as a lad sparred with Freddie Mills and once knocked out the regimental heavyweight champion.

Part of Sangster's secret is that he is a good listener and, thanks to Miss Markie and assistants, and Telexes around the world, a great collator. He has the habit of muttering in head-tilted understanding as you talk, and then pushing a sheet of facts towards you as he gives the answer. One of these shows that the supposed bad year has already yielded 25 Group winners in Europe, another that his horses won over £250,000 in Australia during the spring season alone. He states quite bluntly that he is in the business to make a profit, and that despite the £¼m payday with Detroit and Hortensia at Longchamp last Sunday, this cannot happen by prize money alone.

The system is now well-known and, since they scooped both The Minstrel and Alleged in their first operation in 1975, widely copied. The syndicate, led by Sangster, puts up the loot and goes to the great yearling sales of the world where, on the advice of such geniuses as Vincent O'Brien and that amazing foxy Irishman, Pat Hogan (he wrote his Paris address as "Hotel George Sank"), it

*Robert Sangster,
head of the
furthest-flung racing
empire the world has
ever seen (Gerry
Cranham)*

buys the best-bred and best-looking stock available in the belief that any sort of racecourse success will substantially increase their value.

The ultimate proof of this is that Storm Bird will be worth far more than his million-dollar purchase price even if he gets run over by To Agori Mou this week. "After he had won his second race, I turned down an offer of a hundred thousand pounds for a one-fortieth share in him," says Sangster. "That gave him a value of £4 million, and since he has progressed from there, five million must be his minimum value." But apart from that, the significance of Storm Bird this week is that he is only part of the empire. "Of course I leave everything to Vincent," said Sangster. "He's a genius. Just the same, you don't tell Bart Cummings in Australia, Olivier Douieb in France or Barry Hills in England how to train horses. My job is to be the middle man, to put the right animals and people together and make us, in a very competitive world, come out on top."

The strength forces its way through the narrow-eyed politeness as he makes that point, and you begin to realise a fundamental truth about the man. He may, through his vivacious Australian second wife, Susan, have married his Sheila, but Robert Sangster is nobody's Patsy.

Too many bottles of Chablis in Sangster's lair might sap the spirit. That's when you have to pitch across and talk to someone like Johanna Vardon. Well, you don't actually talk to her. You listen and walk while she takes you round and sorts you out. By the time we had been with her ten minutes there was enough to write the first volume. By the end Chris Smith and I were just shaking our heads in amazement. She was quite a lady.

Non-stop Devotion at the Orphanage
March 8th 1981

If St Francis of Assisi were reincarnated as a woman, many people would bet on his bearing an uncanny resemblance to the tweed skirt and "si-it" dynamism of Barbara Woodhouse. But after seeing an orphan foal on Friday, my money is on the lady with the bottle, Johanna Vardon.

The foal's mother, Miss Mattie, a half-sister to the Oaks winner Altesse Royale, died four hours after giving birth on Thursday. One call to the Mayday number of this foaling season, and the little bay filly was stuffed into a bran sack, put on the back seat of a car and driven the hundred miles from Humberside to a battered old Shropshire farmhouse, where the bottle feeds came every hour and the search for a foster mother continued. Johanna Vardon's National Foaling Bank, started fourteen years ago, had begun to solve its 5,014th case.

The night was not for sleeping for Ms Vardon and her six-girl team. In the next box to where the velvet-nosed orphan lay snug on the straw beneath her heat lamp, another familiar, if riskier, part of the Bank's activities was under way—foaling a "savaging" mare.

"It's 95 per cent the owner's fault," says Johanna with the breezy directness of one who not only practises what she preaches, but builds the pulpits herself. "Owners spoil their mares, make them such precious darlings that when a mare sees a foal in the box she says, 'What is this little brat!' and goes wham! Mares can pick the foals up, throw them around, smash them with their front feet. Our worst case involved five of us staying in the box day and night for three-and-a-half days before she was anywhere near reasonable, but in fourteen years we have never yet failed to get a savaging mare to accept her foal if she has it here."

*Johanna Vardon
bottle-feeds the latest
orphan at the
National Foaling
Bank, 1981 (Chris
Smith)*

Only one girl ("men are no good at this work—can't take it") stayed with the current four-legged baby-basher overnight. "The mare had one go, but she was on a rope, so there was no trouble," said Johanna as the chestnut Arab mare (owned by the alimony-conscious Mrs Khashoggi) stood over her foal, a model of broodiness. "And if we have sorted them out, you will find that in all future foalings they will be perfect mothers."

Since three times as many foals as mares die during birth, finding foster mothers should be easy if people keep the Bank informed, but the adoption process has its problems. "The brood mare arrives with her dead foal—she mustn't lose contact with that," explains Johanna. "Then you take the dead foal out and let the orphan into the adjoining box so that the mare can just see, but can't smell or touch him. She will think, 'Ah, good, my foal has woken up.' Next, skin the dead foal, drape the skin all over the orphan and back him in to where the mare can smell and lick the skin. Take the orphan out, and if the mare panics and frets, you can guarantee the adoption will work."

There are still at least two days of careful coaxing needed before the mare's milk has passed completely through the foal's system, and he then has her smell and the sad little dead-coated charade can be ended. With all that finesse, it's not surprising that Johanna prefers to have orphans at her farm just outside Newport unless they are at a very organised stud, and even then she sometimes travels afar to assist adoption. Stopped for speeding in 1974, she all but melted the stony heart of the law with: "Oh come on, I've got to get to Sandringham to skin a dead foal for the Queen!"

But such royal connections, and even last year's fostering of the full brother to Grundy, does not stop Mrs Baxter (she married last year, but refuses to change her name) being a largely unsung and wholly unsubsidised heroine. Her idea started after an appeal for an orphan foal for her own bereaved pony mare, Flicka, drew a terrific public response: "But everyone said that the breeds wouldn't mix, and it would be too expensive, so I set off and did it entirely voluntarily."

She lived on a regime of two hours' sleep, baked two thousand cakes a week to raise money and guided Flicka's descendants to countless championships in the show ring. Fees had to come, but even now, £7 for an arranged adoption and £28 for a week's boarding are derisory charges and, lithe and spare as the Sadler's Wells dancer she could have become, Johanna Vardon still uses energy as if she were plugged into the mains.

She markets her own patented foal rugs, has published the first *Hunter Stallion Guide* and, following a nasty accident with two of her show champions, has started a nationwide horsebox motorway rescue service. Otherwise, "the humans get taken off in an ambulance, the horses are just stuck." Foal banks have been started in America and Ireland ("Every country should have one"), and as she, the team and the telephone wrestle with more than four hundred cases this spring, an even bigger target beckons.

"I was driving along the M6, and suddenly I was hit by a blinding flash of inspiration," says our latter-day Lady of Assisi. "The sky lit up, and I could see my whole life ahead of me. I shall make this place into an educational trust, raise £200,000 and build a purpose-made unit to both do the job and teach others how." Johanna Vardon is not easily forgotten.

We don't just have orphan foals in racing. A look round
the kids in some yards makes you think that there are
plenty of youngsters who, in a professional sense, are as
motherless as the boys at Barnardo's. In recent years there
has been one certain remedy. Send them to Johnny Gilbert
at the Apprentice School.

What Price their Dreams?
August 16th 1981

Little Eddie O'Donaghue is a sixteen-year-old school-leaver from Middlesbrough. Unlike so many of his contemporaries, he is not unemployed, but there must have been times on Wednesday morning when he wished he was out in the sunshine with the rest of the gang.

For Eddie has now joined a very different academy where lessons are to do with bridging reins, cleaning tack, keeping your heels down, your head up and, if at all possible, one leg on either side of the horse. Little Eddie, the lorry driver's six-stone son who until last month had never sat on a horse, has joined the Racing Apprentices' School and on Wednesday morning was to be seen somersaulting into space as he tried to master the canter.

It had all seemed quite feasible when he practised on the clothes horse under the experienced eye of chief instructor Johnny Gilbert: "Shorten the reins! Hands down! Make him go straight!" But an hour later, pea-on-a-drum atop an ex-racehorse only too aptly named Fast Bowler in Goodwood's big covered ring, it was suddenly not so easy. Gilbert barked: "Canter on!" A fat, wicked-eyed roan pony called Ben gave a plunge one ahead of Eddie, Fast Bowler lurched the other way, and the young O'Donaghue knew the meaning of "solo flight".

It had been just the same the day before, and you had to think that this first stage on the seven-week course was not going well for the crumpled little hopeful from Teesside. But Johnny Gilbert has the warmth, as well as the voice and looks, of Tommy Trinder, and as he put Eddie back up on Fast Bowler the tone was much more the friendly uncle than the super-tough ex-jockey: "Come on now, Edwin, you'll beat him soon. In four weeks' time no one will recognise you." Next day O'Donaghue cantered without trouble.

Turning such unlikely-looking ducklings into something approaching stable-yard swans has been Gilbert's role since 1973, the boys and girls coming some by direct application, others sent on by trainers. To this task Johnny brought not just thirty years of flat, hurdle and (for three nerve-wracked seasons) steeple-chase riding experience, but also a grounding, from the age of eleven, in stablecraft from Stanley Wootton, who is held by many to have been the greatest apprentice trainer of all. Wootton taught his boys from the tenderest age over a number of years within the confines of his highly successful racing stable. Gilbert's boys and girls have to be at least sixteen, and he and his tireless son, Andrew, have just six weeks to work their magic.

The results have been one of the best racing stories of the time. "I can't speak too highly of them," says top Northern trainer Bill Watts, and not just from the considerable riding success of such graduates as Jimmy Bleasdale, 1977 champion apprentice (only previous experience on a Blackpool donkey), Sean Payne, the 1980 Crown Plus Two champion, and Nicky Howe, the current leader.

But now the bad news. A visit to the apprentices' school doesn't just leave you with a soaring heart at the efforts of Eddie and the other young hopefuls. It also leaves you with the taste of anger and despair that in these days of million-dollar stallion syndications, our idea of a basic grounding for young people coming into the industry is still so pitifully small and haphazard. Only a handful of those entering the game get the tuition. Several—like the boy who, despite eighteen months in a stable, had never sat on a horse—are just sent to rectify trainers' negligence, and many more report stories of bad husbandry.

It may be just the chance of location, but at Goodwood, where a gleaming new grandstand straddles the Downs, thanks to a £3 million interest-free loan from the Levy Board, while the apprentice school's stables (funded by the same organisation) huddle in eleven makeshift boxes by the Waterbeach Lodge, it takes a stony mind not to have thoughts about "the rich man in his castle, the poor man at his gate."

At a time when the number of applicants can be as many as forty a week, only sixty lads can be accepted a year, and in conditions that are light years away from the university-campus style the French have at Chantilly. Goodwood was never meant as more than a stopgap after the school's previous home at Stoneleigh had its gallop turned into a grass-testing strip for the Royal Show.

But all is not lost. In that odd, fudging compromise way that some call the British genius, these problems have been recognised, and a massive million-pound appeal has been launched to produce a custom-built school with at least twice the present capacity.

So far the Levy Board has pledged a quarter of a million pounds. Those great philanthropists, Jim Joel and Barnett Shine, found £150,000 between them, but the project now lies becalmed, £20,000 short of the half way point, while a desperate search continues for a site to replace the spot near Newmarket aborted by the dog-in-the-manger objections of the next-door neighbours.

Typically British, perhaps, but at least it's a chance to put one part of racing's house in order. Otherwise, if you don't look after the roots, how can you expect much of a harvest.

The new British Racing School was opened just outside Newmarket in the Autumn of 1983. It's still some way short of the Chantilly campus, but it is smart, and has its own yard, gallops, dormitories and classrooms. Raised mostly by private donations and with a healthy fillip from the Man Power Services Commission, it's a big step forward. But while it's essential that the industry tries to train a better, more informed workforce, the grassroots will always depend fundamentally on the relationship between horses and those who tend them every day.
Stable Lads can be special people. Here's one of them.

Boxing Clever from Stable to Ring
November 15th 1981

They don't just train racehorses at Newmarket. The Suffolk market town where King Charles II launched the Turf as we know it also boasts a group of small but fearsomely fit little men like Dickie McCabe, who at Park Lane's Grosvenor House tomorrow will be taking part in one of the best and worst nights of British sport—the Stable Lads' Boxing Championships.

The bad part is that listening to a thousand £30-a-head dinner-jacketed guests urging diminutive stable lads to knock the living daylights out of each other sometimes makes you think cockfighting is back in favour. But the proceedings raise around £100,000 for the hard-working Stable Lads' Welfare Trust, and anyway, doubts about the atmosphere are not shared by McCabe who, at 27, will be in his seventh final tomorrow, and who, in his professional capacity, led Shergar back in triumph after the Epsom Derby last June.

"They make a bit of noise, but that all helps the occasion for us," says Dickie, whose time with Shergar has made him the richest, as well as the most experienced, lad in action tomorrow. His two-and-half per cent of the colt's record winnings reached £10,000. But just as you begin to picture him as a forelock-tugging time-server, he has a quiet, wide-eyed way of establishing his own credentials. "These championships are no joke, and to win the final (which he has done four times) gives a lot of satisfaction." Suddenly, the soft-bellied observer realises that McCabe is the privileged one.

You might not think that is so when you give him a lift (he has no car) to the modest little rented house he shares on Old Saint's Road; or when you hear that the £67 he takes home from Michael Stoute's successful stable each week is £27 less than he used to get when he left racing to work in a sugarbeet factory for two years. But he remains an achiever.

Like many lads, Dickie originally left his home (in Chesterfield) because the dream of being a jockey was one of the few available to a fifteen-year-old measuring 4ft 11in and weighing only 5st 1lb. His five-year apprenticeship to Mark Prescott showed that this was no Lester Piggott, even if five rides in public did yield a couple of placings, but in his second season he was introduced to boxing and the proudest of all trophies that clutter his living room is a modest-looking little cup for winning an Amateur Boxing Association quarter-final: "I was just a novice stable lad, and I got through to the best in Great Britain. That wasn't bad."

Today he speaks with authority of someone who has won 39 of his 55 fights, and twice been an ABA semi-finalist in his eight stone class. "You have to work hard at your training, but that's the same in any sport, and besides I think these occasions do you good. Before the Derby everybody kept asking how nervous I would feel on the big day, but they forgot that I have boxed in front of thousands of people. I have been on TV and, with Cherry Hinton in the 1978 One Thousand Guineas. I had led up a classic favourite. Why should I be overawed?"

When McCabe starts to talk about "his" horses, you again go into privilege of a high degree. He confides how Shergar had a back problem in February, how his filly Doobie Do "couldn't collect" all season, and how his other colt, Karadar, reared over backwards on him during a stalls test at Newbury.

Even more mature were his comments on Shergar's day of defeat in the St Leger: "When he walked around afterwards, I think he felt he had let everyone down, but how could I be disappointed in him when he had won me two Derbys and a King George? You have to lose sometimes."

But while Dickie is at pains to keep this professional approach, the basic pull that brought him back from the sugarbeet factory will occasionally emerge. "I was very fond of a horse called Ashby Don. He was useless on the racecourse, but he would do anything for me, and he was so good at wriggling out of things that we called him Houdini."

The proprietary nature of this conversation might suggest some resentment between the lad, now hoping to put his Shergar winnings towards a house ("But mortages are difficult on a stable lad's wage"), and the actual owners of his horses. The reply was majestic in its understatement: "I am not resentful. I appreciate a trainer's problems."

Then it was time to buzz down to the New Astley Club, largely founded by the Stable Lads' Welfare Trust, for the final sparring before tomorrow's finals. Dickie's nine rounds include two with his intended opponent, a lanky Kilmarnock eighteen-year-old called Peter Duffy, who moves with the composed aggression of one who has fought for Scotland at junior level. "He likes to go forward, and I am a counter-puncher," said Dickie afterwards, cheekbones jutting pink and sweaty with fatigue, "so it should be a good fight for everyone."

There are times when association with some of the leading figures in either of the two sports with which Dickie is involved can leave you precious close to despair. Listen to McCabe and there has to be hope.

Dickie lost his fight but at least he knows who his opponents are. If you are in the breeding business, the opposition may never look you in the eye. It's called fashion. Step into the ring . . . Ardross.

The Don Juan Syndrome
February 1983

Don't tell Ardross, but his new life as a stallion may not be that easy. It's not the work (forty mares in his first year is the standard quota), but the grim thought that, for all his glorious dual Gold Cup, Horse of the Year racecourse achievements, his success as a stallion is now dependent on his children, and they don't start being, er, started until Tuesday week.

You might assume that in equine terms Ardross is the most eligible bachelor east of *HMS Invincible*. Not so. Desirable, a long way from dirt cheap, but none the less not the very top of the tree. Let's compare prices. Matrimonials with Ardross would set a lady back £13,000 (£6,500 on service, £6,500 on foaling), but with the totally admirable but officially inferior Glint of Gold the cost is £20,000. And if you tryst with last year's brilliant, but little-tested, Derby winner, Golden

Fleece, you need no less than 100,000 Irish punts for the pleasure—a European record.

"What we need is time," said Franca Vittadini on Friday as Ardross, a fraction burlier now than the taut, hard athlete that almost snatched the Arc de Triomphe last October, had his morning constitutional on the lunge rein. Franca is best known for her five victories in Ascot's Diamond Day ladies' race, but as the daughter of Grundy's owner, Dr Carlo Vittadini, she is now, at thirty, in her fourth year as manager of his Beech House Stud at Newmarket, and there is plenty of sense in the blue eyes which laugh behind the long Milanese nose. "Ardross's first foals won't be three-year-olds until 1987," she adds. "So it will be almost 1990 before you can really appreciate how he is doing as a sire."

A paddock away from where Ardross preened was a former Italian Derby winner, a living tribute to the fickleness of breeders' support in the present recession. In 1977, Orange Bay was only inches away from winning Britain's richest race in the blue-and-yellow silks of Franca's father. But when his first two-year-olds appeared in 1981 and failed to score a single success the knockers were out.

For the moment, at least, Ardross has plenty of support. "I thought he was just the sort of animal who ought to go to stud in England," says owner Charles St George, who has put together a syndicate for his £2 million horse that should give at least six year's grace. What's more, in his present circumstances Ardross not only enjoys the life of Riley but has it rather better protected than the rest of us. In 1940 Martin Benson, Beech House's first owner, was so concerned about his great stallion, Nearco, that he built him an air-raid shelter against the *Luftwaffe*, and with the regulation amount of sandbagging, the same hole can surely be proofed against Ronnie and Yuri going berserk.

Ever since Nearco's demise in 1957, proceedings have been watched over by the all-seeing eye of Michael McFarling. "It's a very different rhythm from a training stable," says Michael as he wistfully recalls great horses of the past. "And it takes some horses, and people, a time to adjust. Ardross came to us at the end of October. We then put him out in the field every day until the New Year to give him a complete break. Since then he has been having twelve pounds of corn a day (compared with eighteen pounds when in full race-training)."

During this build-up to the twenty-week covering season, Ardross hasn't had the traditional "trial mare". So how will he cope with the nuptials? "I don't think there will be any problems," says Michael, in the calm, no-giggling way of a man who has spent a lifetime in stud work. "He's a very masculine sort of horse. The more feminine types, like Crepello was, can sometimes spend an hour just looking at a mare, but I don't think Ardross will be long. We've 'teased' him once, and he seemed to have plenty of libido."

When you hear stud people talk in this detached way, and see them poring over the charts which log the most intimate details of every mare visiting their stallions, it's easy to imagine this side of the business as a rather joyless, clinical corner. But if doctors speak coolly, they are not devoid of sympathy. Neither are men like Michael McFarling, and ladies like Franca Vittadini, whose eyes shine as they talk of their horses. When you see that, and when you touch the first velvet-muzzled foals of spring, you appreciate the magic of stud life. And you see why, apart from the potential four-legged goldmines, it can be so attractive to powerful, and not otherwise sentimental, men on whom the game depends for its investment.

It was best put by Omar Sharif when he was still the pin-up of half the universe. Asked why he had got involved in race-horse breeding, "old watery eyes" gave his mostest smile, and said: "To select the mother and the father, and then create a beautiful child—in its little way it's like playing at God."

If acting the Almighty is the attraction, British racing has now been visited by a whole flock of angels from the eastern sky. At a time when the logic and cost of racehorse ownership was becoming beyond the pocket of ordinary English-based mortals, the new oil-financed princes of the Orient have come in and baled us all out. The ruling families of Saudi Arabia, Bahrain, Kuwait and Oman all have enormous investments in studs, horses and stables. Their arrival has been a source of wonder. None more so than the Maktoums of Dubai.

A Classic Case of the Sheikhs
April 24th 1983

News has to gallop fast these days. Within minutes of Wassl winning last Saturday's Greenham Stakes for the Maktoum family, a phone call was put in from Newbury racecourse to Sheikh Mohammed's car on the training grounds. No, not to Newmarket or Lambourn, but to the camel training in mid-desert, back home in Dubai.

It's that sort of keenness which could make the coming week the start of a quite astonishing year for this ruling family of that tiny oil and trading state on the Persian Gulf. In Thursday's One Thousand Guineas, the French filly Ma Biche will carry the colours of Sheikh Mohammed's older brother, Maktoum al Maktoum, as favourite for this first Classic of the season and in Saturday's Two Thousand Guineas, Wassl will carry the yellow silks of younger brother Ahmed. And we are already only five weeks away from the Oaks and Derby in which Sheikh Mohammed's Ghaiya and Dunbeath are leading fancies.

Racing empires are nothing new. At least three—Sangster, Niarchos and the Aga Khan—currently vie with the Maktoum involvement. But never have a family set their cap at the British racing scene with such total, extravagant relish.

Six years ago they had just one horse; three seasons back, still only a few dozen. Today the count stretches to no fewer than 238 horses in training, three studs, sixty broodmares, shares in almost every top stallion and plans afoot to take another stud in Ireland. You could almost think that the family were bent on buying every descendant of those first imported Arab stallions which became the founding fathers of the thoroughbred three centuries ago.

Confronted by such figures, it's natural to grab the calculator and boggle at facts like £40,000 a week on training fees, and over fifty million dollars spent at the American yearling sales alone. But all that is just bad for the eyeballs. What we are facing is infinite wealth, incomes of several millions of pounds a day, and so the question is not how they afford it but why. And the best answer is found not in their lavish houses and hotel suites in Britain, but out in Dubai on the camel track.

Camel racing may sound a bit of a laugh over here, and it's true that the sight of the runners at the start, lined up but lying down, is something of a culture shock, as indeed is the enormous fully railed ten kilometre circuit, and the titchy Bedouin jockey boys. But one afternoon at the races with Sheikh Mohammed in full Arab dress shows you how seriously the sport is taken.

At the biggest international camel meeting earlier this month, Dubai carried off all four classics. Such a clean sweep over here would break every record book, and as the summer scene shifts to the British Turf, the interest is no less quick. "We have always known horses," said Sheikh Mohammed, after flying in on Friday with his brothers Hamdan and Ahmed. "We understand them and like them, but at times it is still like being in someone else's house. So it is especially good if they win."

The house which shelters Wassl, one of the fourteen training stables patronised by the family, is that of John Dunlop in the very shadow of Arundel Castle in Sussex. It was raw and cold on Wednesday morning, and the talk was not of empires but of the battle up ahead. How, for instance, Wassl, with just two races behind him, might cope with the power of Gorytus and Diesis (who worked well yesterday) over Newmarket's straight, pitiless mile of grass.

With Danzatore's defection on Friday, and question marks still hanging over Gorytus and Diesis, a solid practical witness is needed. Come forward Chris Blyth, 33-year-old tough, uncompromising Scottish stable lad and chief second to Wassl, just as he was to Sheikh Mohammed's Scottish Derby winner, Jalmood, last year, and that first horse, Hatta, back in 1977. "People say my horse is inexperienced," says Chris, stroking Wassl's dark satin neck. "But they forget he was ready and winning on a racecourse last June, well ahead of any of his rivals. And while he had some troubles last year (a pulled muscle) he's two hundred-per-cent now. He'll win the Guineas and Derby, whether the others are fit or not."

Chris doesn't have a phone in his car. If Wassl wins on Saturday, he won't even want one. For the two of them will be at the very heart of the Empire.

*If you look at all the different types of people in this section
you might think that there are as many ways of training a
racehorse as skinning a cat. Mercifully, puss would be
quite safe with most of these because you don't find many
successes in animal training who don't end up liking all
animals a bit—sorely as some of them may have been tried.
Take our first example—a man who must in his time have
had as much reason for cursing the equine race as anyone
since the Mexicans got duped by Cortes 400 years ago.*

Darkie and Charlie and The Dikler
March 1973

They are the sort of thick, sure hands that you would like to see above you on a
mountain rope, but towards 3.30 next Thursday afternoon, they will wring
helplessly with a heavier involvement than anyone in the huge tense crowd
awaiting the start of the Cheltenham Gold Cup.

These are the horseman's hands of "Darkie" Deacon, and it is because of their
extraordinary strength and understanding that the 43-year-old stableman will on
Thursday be in the unique position of having the two horses he looks after in
Fulke Walwyn's Lambourn yard competing in the supreme championship race—
and both are leading hopes to resist the odds-on claims of Walwyn's neighbour
and former jockey, Fred Winter, with Pendil.

When both The Dikler, four years ago, and Charlie Potheen, eighteen months
ago, arrived at the lime and white stables where the 1962 Gold Cup hero
Mandarin is still a loved-for pet, their reputation for intractable brilliance had
preceded them. "Both of them had won point-to-points, but both of them had
also run out," says Walwyn. "So I thought I had better give them to Darkie, and
he's done a marvellous job on them. He's taught Charlie to settle, but The Dikler
can really pull, and it is very, very hard work for a man to ride him every
morning."

Part of Walwyn's complete mastery of his craft is that he can retain and use the
skills of a man such as Deacon. But all this should not lead you to imagine Darkie
as a fifteen-stone muscle man specially employed to anchor runaway point-to-
pointers. For although the face is weathered by 10,000 downland mornings (this
with his black hair brings the nickname), the rest of the body is small and almost
bird-like. He is only 8st 5lb now, and passed Grade 3 medical for the Army
through being underweight and having a skull fracture at the age of twelve.

A Swindon boy, he was apprenticed to Ossie Bell at Lambourn, but arrived a
few months after Tommy Gosling, who went on to be a star apprentice and
jockey, and therefore took most of the likely rides.

"But I got quite a bit of riding wherever I went, yet every time I looked like
riding a winner something went wrong. Once I was due to ride a really good

Darkie Deacon, double-handed, with The Dikler (left) and Charlie Potheen, March 1973 (Frank Hermann)

horse, Fairy Fulmer, at Epsom, and my mother died the day before. "Then there was one time when I got beat a neck at Chepstow and should have won. But it was Easter Monday, and I had been serving as officers' mess cook in the Army until Saturday. I don't think it was exactly the ideal preparation."

As with many men before him with families to feed (wife Joyce, and three sons), a period of some disillusionment set in when the race riding finally ended; and he went to work for two years' as a fitter's mate at Aldermaston. "It was better money, but I was away from home twelve hours a day, and when the lads got a bit of a pay rise, I came back. Then I got a job for the guv'nor and I've been there fifteen years."

The basic pay today of £20 a week, even with generous bonuses for winners in a successful yard like Walwyn's, is still far from princely. But if you look at the enthusiasm in those clear blue eyes when he comes to talk of the horses he has done, you feel that he's taken a lot more than mere money out of the job. "There was Some Alibi—he did win at Cheltenham; but Exhibit A, he would have won the Champion Hurdle if the ground had been hard. And then there was Irish Imp—he was a really lovely horse, nearly my favourite of all."

For each of those stars, he has won awards for turn-out, and has repeated the achievement with his present two. These and action photos of them adorn the neat little semi on the Lambourn housing estate. But for all the immaculate preparation in the afternoon, the real work is in the morning. And even before the horses leave their boxes, you can appreciate the sheer size of Darkie's task. Charlie is a wiry 16.2 hands with a lovely ear-pulling disposition in the box, but all action once a gallop is on. "In fact, in a race you virtually cannot hold him at all to start with. But I can hold him all right just as long as I don't shorten the reins. He's okay now, but early on he used to turn round suddenly and try and come home, and I hit him once and he just set off hell for leather."

Those problems, enough to defeat most riders, pale into insignifance beside those posed by The Dikler. For this is an enormous 17.1 hands horse with massive power and a temperament which at times reminds you of a caged tiger. "When he first came, he would rear a lot and twice came over backwards with me. But now you can humour him, though if he wants to he still can just take off with you."

The soft Wiltshire voice has no false modesty in it when he says: "You know, he's the only horse that's ever been able to do that to me. But if he wins on Thursday, I'll forgive him, and if Charlie does, I might even forgive him for dropping me early in the season!"

Darkie had his moment all right, that Cheltenham of 1973. Charlie Potheen didn't make it but The Dikler did, sprinting up to snatch the Gold Cup from Pendil in the final hundred yards. These old horses have met their maker now but Darkie is still at Saxon House, 25 years of priceless service behind him and the responsibilities of Head Lad now on his rock hard shoulders.
Our next hero is made of more volatile stuff. In fact, the training game has never seen anything quite like Maurice Zilber. Here is the tale of how he saddled Empery to win the 1976 Derby for Lester Piggott.

Zilber's Walks on Water
June 6th 1976

Maurice Zilber sat in his hotel room on Derby eve and read the evening newspaper. He saw Lester Piggott's column headlined: I Will Need a Gun to Stop Wollow. He reached for the phone, and when the silence at the other end indicated that the Epsom maestro was on the line, Zilber said: "Lookka Lester, thissa Wollow he no wonder horse. My horse, he cumma good. You needa no gun tomorrow, thissa Empery he going to win."

According to the Zilber script, Lester replied: "Well, you are probably right—as usual." But whatever Piggott's reservations on Derby Day, he at least knew that he was going out to do battle on an animal primed for the big time by a master of his craft.

And if that claim is singularly uncluttered by false modesty, it only makes the story of the fifty-year-old Egyptian-born Chantilly-based trainer even better in the telling: "I amma different from the others. I amma gambler. In Egypt I amma toppa trainer twelve times. Then Nasser come and I havva nothing. I cumma to Paris, I amma skeent, but I watchaa the horses and in two months I makka the money. I trainna for Wildenstein. I toppa de leest three times. But Mr Wildenstein and I disagree. I have Mr Hunt cumma to me. And again I winna all da bigga races."

Under such a fusillade there is always a tendency to think that much of it is rubber bullets. But for the record, Zilber had consistently said Empery would take the Derby this year, and he first told us last October on an excruciating morning when the stormy partnership with Bunker Hunt was in one of its deepest troughs, and trainer and ten-gallon-hatted owner stalked up and down at different ends of the string.

Last Wednesday Empery was as good as his trainer's word and, in hindsight, the form adds up. He had been fourth in the French Guineas, only fifth next time after coughing, but was clearly on the way back when third in the one-and-a-quarter-mile Prix Lupin. Presented at Epsom with a mile and a half and really good ground for the first time, Empery made the predictions come true.

If the horse was primed, so too was Piggott—to a mental and physical peak extraordinary even by his own towering standards. For the Derby really does mean a lot to Lester. You see it among the mementoes at his home, you find it among the six Derby-winning jockeys in his blood and you couldn't miss it in his radiant, boyish victory mood at Epsom on Wednesday.

Yet the most emotion I have ever seen him show was after Cavo Doro finished second to Morston three years ago. He also bred that horse, and sitting over his meal that evening he looked as if he had had a million years of bereavements. The wrinkled skin seemed to be fading into the skull, and he just kept muttering: "That would have been the record, but the ground was too firm, too firm."

That was one of the times that I thought Piggott's physical resources had come to the end of their tether, and although he has continued to climb new heights since then, I believe that it is no coincidence that the finest achievements have come after short breaks from the saddle.

Two years ago a difference of opinion with the French rules saw him off on a few days' Riviera holiday. He followed that with one of the most astonishing "charges" in his whole career—45 winners in 24 racing days. Last year's enforced rest preceeded his nine-winner Royal Ascot blitz, and last week again we had the Longchamp stewards to thank for seeing to it that the maestro polished his tan at Antibes.

On Wednesday Piggott's talent was at its brightest. The razor-sharpness to seize a good place from the start, the radar-like guidance through the jostling of Tattenham Corner and the drawing-the-bow patience for the final arrowing run home. To say that Dettori on Wollow suffered by comparison is to avoid kicking ourselves for not fully appreciating this beforehand; and more important, for not discerning the two biggest question marks that hung over Wollow.

The first was that the Two Thousand Guineas form, which he reproduced to the pound with Vitiges, has not worked out well, and the second was that except in the Two Thousand Guineas Wollow has tended to be a slow starter.

In the Derby he reverted to that habit, and was immediately in trouble trying to avoid being cut off from his inside draw. So contrary to all public clamour it was not a race that Wollow lost, but one that Empery and Piggott won.

After several years of close association with Piggott, who is now forty, I am sure that the gunfighter analogy fits him best. From a very early age—he rode his first winner when he was twelve—he has been able to do this one thing supremely well to make his way in the world. It is fired by a wild hunger for winning that drives him to take on anyone to get to the top. On the way, the wildness has sometimes spilled over, but it has always been tempered by a ferocious gunman's discipline which knows that only the steadiest hand shoots straight.

Maybe there is something else. In expansive mood on Friday, Maurice Zilber flashed those brown Egyptian eyes, and said: "You wanta knowa my secret? I can walk onna water." Last week was only the latest evidence that Lester, too, can do without the boat.

Zilber and Piggott may be odd-balls but they still hail from the standard racing locations of Chantilly and Newmarket. The fun of racing, particularly National Hunt, is that the big plans can be hatched all over. Let's go to the West Country early in 1977.

Oliver Carter out West
January 1977

Rolling blazing barrels of tar down the main street on Guy Fawkes Day has for long been the most exciting annual event in the little Devonshire market town of Ottery St Mary. But if local horse hero Otter Way fulfils the dreams of local farmer Oliver Carter, these "No Popery" bunfights are likely to be outshone. If the plan works, Otter Way won't just become the first Devon horse to win the Cheltenham Gold Cup—he will also take the Grand National and then cross the Channel to win the French Grand National, which at £59,000 to the winner is the world's richest steeplechase.

You may think that this bid to become the most famous Ottery St Mary product since Samuel Taylor Coleridge dreamed of the Ancient Mariner up at his father's vicarage is a bit ambitious for a horse who has run only six steeplechases in his nine-year-old life, and hasn't been seen in public since last June. But then, you haven't spoken to his 58-year-old owner, trainer, breeder and exercise rider Oliver Carter, who says cheerfully: "People can laugh at me if they like, but I honestly don't see too much trouble because, believe me, nobody knows how good this horse is yet."

People had their share of ridiculing Mr Carter's end-of-the-rainbow ambitions last year. First, when he ran Otter Way in the Gold Cup just five days after winning in slightly less competitive company at the South Devon Point-to-Point; and secondly, when he answered their patronising congratulations for Otter Way's respectable seventh place with the blunt comment, "I was disgusted with him." But it is in the nature of Oliver Carter and his horse to get the last laugh, and Otter Way then proceeded to win £16,163 in his next three races, ending with the Whitbread Gold Cup in record time and the *Horse and Hound* Cup at Stratford after being unridden for three weeks because of back trouble.

"It was a warble that had worked its way through to his back," explained Oliver. "I couldn't put a saddle on him at all, and had to train him on the lunge." Such rural problems don't seem to bother Carter much. He's a man who was too busy with cattle even to sit on a horse until he was forty, and then he made the first two racehorses he owned successful. One of them, Overcourt, won a big race at Cheltenham. He is a farmer, and Otter Way received his early education in the hunting field, and his first racing experience in the point-to-point world, where he remains unbeaten after twelve appearances.

"In fact, I was out hunting on him last Saturday," said Carter. "And he has been out enough times to qualify for a hunter certificate, so that I can always run him back in hunter 'chases if he doesn't come off in the big time. But I don't think it'll be necessary because he is better than ever this year. I let him have a real long holiday after Stratford. He did not come in out of the field until the end of October, and you know he is already the talk of the West Country."

We will have the first chance to judge Otter Way's progress when he runs against Royal Frolic at Wincanton on 3 February under the powerful driving of Jeff King. But for further clues it is worth listening to his original partner, Grant Cann, unbeaten on the horse in nine point-to-points and two hunter 'chases: "I rode him in a piece of work on Thursday, and he was better than he's ever been at this time of year. Last year he had become a real man, but this time he is like a sergeant-major. With his jumping now really together, I think he could beat anything."

Our hero was bred out of the £10 union between the premium stallion, Salmonway Spirit, and the unraced mare, Marquita, whose origins are unregistered and whose purchase was equally casual. "I found her out on Dartmoor," says Carter happily. "I was buying forty head of cattle, and she was running in among them. So I took her as well. Gave £125 for her. And she was in foal, too," adds South Devon's answer to Daniel Wildenstein.

Carter has got eight horses and a staff of three about the place, and claims that his success is due to old-fashioned methods: "We just give them oats and bran and a lot of chaff. I haven't fed nuts in years, and I wouldn't know a steroid if I ate one."

There are two sorts of people in racing, those who get involved because beyond everything else they get enormous fun out of the game, and those who can't turn any corner without worrying how it will affect their already-overladen pockets. After a talk with men like Oliver Carter, you don't have any doubts who in real terms will remain the richer.

Sadly Otter Way lit no bonfires in 1977 but it was typical of the horse and of his owner that they were still going strong in 1983 when Otter Way won the prestigious Horse and Hound Cup as an evergreen 15-year-old. They are just another example that the game has always been as much a test of the spirit as anything else. So perhaps the idea of a trainer in a wheel-chair isn't so strange after all. 1981 was officially designated "The Year of the Disabled" and a trip to the Curragh was needed to see it so.

A Wheelchair Assault
January 11th 1981

Don't cluck in sympathy. There was more warning than wishful thinking in Michael O'Brien's voice last Friday as he looked up at Bright Highway from his wheelchair and said: "This is my year, the Year of the Disabled, and I am going to win the Gold Cup."

Since he has already trained the big bay horse to win the Mackeson and Hennessy Gold Cups and so become favourite for the Cheltenham championship, Michael's is no idle boast. But if you wanted odds on it that March night in Columbia Hospital, South Carolina, seven years ago when they told him he would never walk again, you would have had to start counting the pine trees in Dakota. Within a week O'Brien would all but die of a blood clot, and his elder brother Leo and intended right-hand man would then suffer a skull fracture which has left permanent hearing damage. Indeed Bright Highway himself has needed two throat operations before blossoming to his present stardom.

But you cannot argue with 63 winners in three full training seasons. You just make the trip to the Curragh's sheep-and-gorse-sprinkled plain in County Kildare to see the extraordinary O'Brien operation ticking over. Bright Highway was really no better than expected. With plenty of flesh on him after his midwinter break and no fences to draw one of those great crowd-gasping leaps, he hacked gently around like some big heavyweight lolling through an easy day in the gym. Leo was as painstakingly attentive both in the yard and out on the gallops as legend suggested, but the real amazement is to watch Michael wheel himself on to the fork lift attachment to his van. Fifteen whirring, sliding seconds later he and the wheelchair are secured at the van controls watching the horses file past. Up on the gallops the performance is done in reverse and like some little

Michael O'Brien out with his string on The Curragh in January 1981 (Chris Smith)

crumpled gnome Ireland's most unlikely trainer watches, instructs and queries his team.

With a name like O'Brien you might imagine that Michael and Leo were bred for the job. But the illustrious Vincent was no relation. Their father was a boiler in Cadbury's chocolate factory at Newcastle, County Dublin, and they were just two of his nine children who only met up with horses when Leo went to work on the local farm of trainer and breeder "Toss" Taafe. A limited career as jockeys began in Ireland, before they tried their luck in America.

"Out in America I knew I had to prove myself. I quit smoking, got really fit and with the chance of riding for a fine trainer like Jonathan Sheppard, and some good owners, I had been champion jockey and was on top of the job when the accident came."

Of course those satisfied customers, most notably the Corinthian figure of Bright Highway's owner George Strawbridge, were able to rally round when the seriousness of Michael's condition was realised. But the parable of the talents works for goodwill and insurance money too, and the measure of Michael's success is that while it was the American connection which set him up, four years later fewer than a third of his 25 horses are US owned. And it's no one-star outfit. At this year's festival O'Brien may be able to field highly-rated contenders Seanogue, Tacroy, Little Water and Sidney Parade in addition to Bright Highway making his Gold Cup bid.

When you search for the secret beyond the obvious deep horse understanding of both brothers, and the vast stable-side contribution of Leo, you find it in the odd challenging remarks with which Michael stakes out his conversation. "I would have been a success at anything I decided on." "I don't rate any trainer better than me." "I may be in a wheelchair but they know who's the boss."

Three weeks after the accident things looked pretty black for the crippled jockey—a new house with a heavy mortgate and wife Ann already pregnant with Joanne's little sister Anne Marie. "I was so depressed I wouldn't speak to anyone," he says. "They sent a psychiatrist in to explain that I had to come to terms with everything. He went on so long I got mad, mad to show everyone that I could win through."

That "madness" doesn't always lead to popularity amongst the Irish racing family. "Some people don't like me but I like that," says Michael. "It shows they're worried about me as a rival, not as a cripple." But the "madness" is also a central force in his major victory of mind over matter.

Michael O'Brien gives that sideways triumphant grin again. "In some ways I think I have an advantage on other trainers. Travelling is difficult for me, so I just sit here in the office plotting and planning. And believe me when I have got a horse really prepared for a race I don't mind if the Almighty takes us on."

Bright Highway injured himself and couldn't run at Cheltenham but Michael O'Brien continued to defy his difficulties and won the 1982 Irish Grand National and with it the National Hunt Trainer's title. Back at the start of '81, another set of problems. What happens to flat racers in the winter? Particularly those classic hopes who are going to attract acres of newsprint in a couple of months' time? Guy Harwood had the answers.

The Weight of the Matter
February 1981

If you are one of his considerable band of supporters, you may be disturbed to hear that only two months away from the most important race of his life, Britain's most valuable athlete is still seventy pounds overweight.

Drink, sloth or sheer greed? No, forget the alarums. To-Agori-Mou, seven million dollars' worth of thoroughbred classic hope, is alive and well and working on schedule in rural England at Pulborough, Sussex. But don't forget the weight, because it is a key component in what has long been one of the most fascinating challenges in British sport, to get a horse ready for the Two Thousand Guineas at Newmarket so early in the season (2 May this year).

Consider the problem. By the end of the flat-racing season in November, you know that you have a leading two-year-old colt, the equivalent of an eighteen-year-old human athlete. You also know that because of his breeding (in this case, To-Agori-Mou is by the sprinter Tudor Music), he is unlikely to last out the mile-and-a-half jackpot of the Epsom Derby. So by Two Thousand Guineas day your equine athlete, barely 21 in human terms, has to be at his peak, having had to survive the winter without exchanging one word with you.

Which is where we came in. For while the problem and the basic training methods to solve it haven't changed a lot, in the past the only means of assessment was the trainer's eye and ear. Those judgments remain the final arbiters, but the present-day trainer also uses contemporary sources of evidence. If a horse looks heavier, by how much? If it has lost a few pounds, how many?

At 42, Guy Harwood is very much a modern trainer and, with Recitation and Kalaglow in support of To-Agori-Mou, he has the strongest classic hand at the

A change of diet? The subsequent 2,000 Guineas winner, To-Agori-Mou, samples trainer Guy Harwood's jacket in February 1981 (Gerry Cranham)

moment. His brisk factual line of attack is more like his father's engineering world than the often happily imprecise racing circus, and in the early days (he started with fifteen jumpers in 1966) there were some old sweats who used to disparage his approach. But with Young Generation, Ela-Mana-Mou and Rankin placed in classic races in the past two years, and with seventy winners of almost £250,000 last season, it is now accepted that Harwood is not just clear-sounding theory, but undeniably-accomplished fact.

Tall, lean and boyishly active, Harwood rides on the gallops, coat billowing, with his horses. "He looks like Batman," giggled daughter Amanda disloyally. He enjoys shooting down racing fallacies: "The biggest myth is that a three-year-old is going to be a whole lot bigger and heavier than it was as a two-year-old. That's nonsense. If you find his best racing weight, you will discover that as a three-year-old it is almost exactly the same. If he is much heavier, he is unfit. If he is lighter, he is sick."

So how unfit is To-Agori-Mou, who turned the scales at 1,160 pounds last week compared with 1,090 when he gave Vincent O'Brien's Irish ace, Storm Bird, a battle royal in the Dewhurst Stakes last October? Not a lot, to judge by the ease with which he came through a long trot and three uphill spins on Wednesday morning. But across his shoulder, and along his neck, you could see that the trainer still had plenty to work on, and the same applies to Recitation and Kalaglow. At 1,160 pounds Recitation, who will be aimed at the French classics, is thirty pounds above the weight which won him last year's Grand Criterion, and the unbeaten but much lighter-framed Kalaglow ("must be the Derby horse") is also thirty pounds above his best weight of only 1,040.

All this emphasis on weight makes one wonder when each racecourse will be equipped with a weighbridge, and the horse's racing weight be known to the public, just as it is in greyhound racing. It is a crucial statistic which would do more for our knowledge of a horse's fitness than all the quotes and excuses.

The excess weight first went on To-Agori-Mou and his fellows after they had their shoes removed, and were exercised on lunge rein for three weeks at the end of the season and then began cantering again at Christmas. "They are out for one-and-a-half hours, but it is not fast work, just conditioning," Harwood says. "But from now on we will begin to sharpen up, and although they eat as much as they want, we will get the weight off to be within ten pounds of their best when they reappear."

You will appreciate that while Guy Harwood has built up his own methods, some of the most striking ideas are borrowed from the best places. When he was starting up, he bought a horse called Mars, which was trained by Vincent O'Brien: "He was very charming and showed me round. It was the time of Nijinsky, and Vincent already had a woodchip gallop and a weighing machine. They seemed to make sense."

Picking up a classic trainer's idea and training a classic winner, are very different things. But with Guy Harwood it is now only a question of when.

The prediction may have been easy but Harwood justified it to the ounce. Having been 1160 lbs when the piece was written, To-Agori-Mou reappeared on April 14 weighing 1105 lbs and was beaten. On May 2nd, weighing 1090 lbs (his previous year's racing weight), he won the Two Thousand Guineas . . . QED. A year later now—training calculations of another kind. And just as vital.

Mattie McCormack and the Horse who Paid Off
June 13th 1982

Life-savers come in many forms, but maybe none more exciting than the horse which delivers when the money is down. That's why there will be a special gleam of gratitude beneath trainer Mattie McCormack's angled ginger eyebrows when the two-year-old Horage parades before Royal Ascot's Coventry Stakes on Tuesday.

For last September, towards the end of McCormack's none-too-successful second season with a licence, he splashed out £42,000 for eight yearlings at Doncaster Sales, only for the promised owners to renege on the deal. "How I survived, I will never know," says 42-year-old Mattie in a voice that still clings to

Mattie McCormack ponders what would have happened if Horage (left) had not starred in 1982 (Chris Smith)

its County Carlow birthplace. "There was no way I could go on taking it financially, and the next seven months seemed like seven years."

The one gleam of hope during that period was the flowing stride and alert white-blazed head of Horage, who at 8,000 guineas is the most expensive of the thirteen horses in McCormack's little yard at Sparsholt, near Wantage, Oxfordshire. "Once he had been broken, I knew he had something," says Mattie, savouring the tale like a drinking man at a desert oasis. "You know what a good horse is like when you get on them, they can operate. So when I really wanted to find out, I rode him myself."

The little man's self-confidence comes not from glamorous years on the tracks as a jockey, but from breezy mornings as one of the best work riders in the business. Originally apprenticed at Wetherby as a fifteen-year-old, McCormack then became a lad at some of the best stables in the land—Boyd-Rochfort, Murless, Van Cutsem, Peter Walwyn—and had ridden gallops on such champions as Welsh Pageant, Mysterious and Grundy. He recalls with relish the day he "found out" about Grundy: "He worked with a reasonable three-year-old who at the weight-for-age scale should have been giving him two stone. Instead, Grundy gave him a stone-and-a-half, and cantered at him. Grundy had to be some horse, and we made some money when he ran."

At that time, Mattie was saving up for the day he branched out on his own. This season, with Horage, he was defending his hard-won corner, and it is not surprising that he used the Grundy "system" to make sure about his own two-year-old hopeful. "I have a three-year-old called Shiny Hour who won last year and ran in some decent races," says Mattie. "So at the beginning of March, I rode Horage against him with the weight the wrong way round for the two-year-old. We went four-and-a-half furlongs up Barry Hills's gallop, and Horage treated Shiny Hour like a selling plater. Then I knew we were on."

But it is one thing to be sure you have a horse that can run, another to find a race you are certain you can win, and a vital third to keep the secret away from prying eyes and greedy pockets. The chosen target was the unsung Hillhouse Stakes at Ayr on 30 March, the first Tuesday of the flat-racing season. "I had picked it as long ago as January," says Mattie proudly. "They wouldn't know me up in Scotland, and you can get a bet on up there. My staff knew Horage could go, but they were told to keep their mouths shut and they would be looked after. They all did, and they were."

The price they got was 6–1 which, if it seemed generous as Horage drew away from his field on that first occasion, has subsequently looked like the "steal" of the century as the colt has forged clear in all his four other races, including the five-length defeat of the flying Brondesbury, who has won his other five races by an aggregate of over 52 lengths. There is still no knowledge the limit of Horage's ability for, by Tumble Wind out of a Sicambre mare, he is bred to get much farther than Tuesday's six furlongs, and if he thrives he can even go beyond this season's two-year-old races to the Classics next year.

Such giddy thoughts come back to the loft as Mattie's wife Hilda pauses for coffee in the little house at the end of the yard. The eighteen boxes outside are a long way from the hundred-horse strings of the big-league trainers. The yellow Racing Calendars on Hilda's desk in the corner are far from the telexes and switchboards of the million-dollar operation, and for sure the room for man-oeuvre is far less than those high-flying colleagues have who will soon be jetting to Kentucky in search of new equine talent.

Three of the eight "unwanted" two-year-olds remain unsold and, although the six winners recorded so far are half the season total McCormack has set himself, there remains the feeling that Horage's achievements still represent only a fingerhold on public attention. Maybe, but when the little man from County Carlow decks himself out in topper and tails on Tuesday, there won't be a prouder being in Christendom. He has climbed a long way already.

Despite an injured foot Horage duly won at Ascot next week and then continued on his way to notch up nine successes in a row and push his trainer firmly into the limelight.
Another trainer now, and at first blush about as complete a contrast to Mattie McCormack as you could ever get. For this young man could never have an anonymous start. His problems would always be the measurement of himself against the name his father gave him. He was the son of Vincent O'Brien.

An Irish Heir Asserts Class
August 1982

The heir apparent is his own man. That, more than easy jibes about "silver spoons", is the truth about the extraordinary emergence of 26-year-old David O'Brien as a trainer to rival the legendary achievements of his father Vincent O'Brien, whose horses have for a generation won everything bar the Boat Race.

At York last Tuesday, David's Assert ran clean away from his rivals in the £80,000 Benson and Hedges Golden Cup and even the most hardened profes-sionals had to admit that for all his guilded connections this was no ordinary second season trainer.

Assert, already the winner of the French and Irish Derbys, had been brought back from a testing defeat at Ascot to win superbly over a shorter distance in a race renowned for beaten favourites. Four days earlier the stable's Pas de Seul had won the prestigious Hungerford Stakes at Newbury on his first public appear-ance since fracturing a cannon bone at exercise last September.

These are the sort of achievements we associate with O'Brien senior's hey-day; and since both David's horses sported Robert Sangster's green and blue silks, carried by the Vincent-trained Golden Fleece in this year's Epsom Derby, the assumption of some sort of cloning of style becomes obvious.

And when you learn that David still lived in his parent's palatial Tipperary home, kept his fifty-odd horses less than a mile away, and shared part of the famous Ballydoyle gallop as well as his father's Garboesque aversion to interviews, the assumption seemed a certainty.

It's not something you will get agreed if you finally beat your way down the long winding lane to the still-unfinished white-stone stabling block. "My father has been a marvellous inspiration," says David in his shy but beguiling brogue. "But since I leave the house every morning at 5.30 to see my horses and don't get back till eight at night you can hardly say that I am in his pocket." He added with his easy laugh; "Anyway he's only looked at my horses once since the spring."

With his tousled blond hair, scuffed blue jeans and lumberjack boots, David looks a far cry from his immaculate father and is clearly seeking direct physical involvement rather than any "son of the house" command. "I believe in feeding them myself, morning and evening," he says, making light of the task. "That way I can be sure of how they have spent the night and I train them a lot according to how they are eating. I like to be around them as much as I can because I think that a lot of the going racing and the socialising take you away from your horses and the whole idea must be for the trainer to get inside their heads."

This almost monastic dedication has so impressed Assert's owner, Robert Sangster, that he now has shares in 37 of the 51 horses David trains and has offered to set him up in England if ambition stretches across the water. Equally convinced is stable jockey Christy Roche, who had previously served fifteen years with the late great Paddy Prendergast. "This guy is something else," says Christy. "He has a whole new modern style of training and his attention to detail is amazing. After Assert won the French Derby every other horse at Ballydoyle got the cough, but David put Assert into another unfinished yard, kept two lads, who went nowhere else, and even changed his own clothes night and morning to feed the horse. For six weeks. Assert missed the cough."

More surprising still is that six years ago few would have thought it possible of David, who had followed school at Ampleforth with four years' accountancy in Dublin. "I was the assistant at Ballydoyle at that time," says Michael Dickinson, now Britain's star National Hunt trainer. "David used to come down at weekends and obviously took some interest. But you never used to see him around the yard and nobody expected him to get involved like this."

And even after David had begun learning his craft, doing spells in America, Australia (where he noticed that Melbourne trainer Tommy Hughes fed the horses himself) and with his father, many still did not realise the mettle of the man. "Perhaps he was a bit overawed by all the 'wise men,' in Vincent's stable," says Sangster. "But, once he was on his own, the dedication was astonishing. He has only been four nights away from Ballydoyle since January and one of those, my wife's birthday party at Newmarket, he only agreed to come if the plane took him back (to the private airstrip beside Vincent's gallop) at 7 o'clock next morning. My only worry is that he might graft too hard."

Back with the horses, David retreats behind his shrugging laugh and denies both a lack of plan and overwork. "I always knew I would go training," he says. "But I wanted to do something else first, another discipline. As for strain," he adds with blue eyes shining under the suntan, "we have some wonderful horses and I just love being with them. Why, in the winter we had one week of fierce snow, eight foot of it all round the yard. Nobody could get here. The water was frozen. So there were four of us, and we had to get fifty horses out in the centre of the yard and get water up by tractor. But the job is to get it done somehow."

Of course, there is still a long way to go and much to prove. Some may still say that David O'Brien's meteoric start is the ultimate case of a rich boy's beginners' luck. Others, more charitably, may recall the parable of the talents. But those closest to him will think only of the "amazing attention to detail". And that, whatever the style, means like father, like son.

Assert's attempt at the Arc De Triomphe got bogged down in a real Parisian deluge but David O'Brien's place in big time was finally established on June 6th 1984 when he saddled Secreto to win the Epsom Derby. More than that, the horse he beat, in a dramatic photo finish, was the brilliant 2000 guineas winner, El Gran Senor. That made it a family affair. El Gran Senor was trained by Vincent O'Brien.
If one great torch seemed to be ready for a relight in the summer of '82, another was soon to be doused for ever. So we trekked down to Findon for the best free show in the business.

Captain's Stable
August 1982

His bark may now be worse than his bite. He may be hitting seventy this month, and retiring at the end of the season, but the good news for racegoers is that trainer Ryan Price has a bit of woof in him yet.

With that magnificent chiselled face, and the cheekily tilted hat, Ryan was born to be centre-stage, and the thought that he might suddenly exit left was more than we ordinary theatre lovers could stand. But the past week has revealed, as freely predicted, that the Price retirement will be partial at best. After two seasons with horses ravaged by virus, the only Englishman in recent years to have won classic races on the Flat and over jumps is making way for his bright Irish assistant, Con Horgan, but will remain and advise from his home below the Sussex yard where he has trained these last ten years.

Of course Price has been in the game a lot longer than that. "Fifty-eight years," he said on Friday before characteristically answering the question begged. "Rode my first winner in a point-to-point when I was twelve years old. Was so light that I had to carry six-and-a-half stone of lead. Been a marvellous life. Wouldn't have missed an effing thing. Fun, real fun." Like the man, the pitch of the stories which come flooding out varies from whispering grandee to bawling gipsy.

The racing story is easiest told. The training triumphs: over jumps, the three Champion Hurdles, the Gold Cup, the Grand National and the notoriety of those four controversial Schweppes Hurdles, which involved suspension after Rosyth's second victory and the discovery that Hill House made his own "dope". On the Flat, the Oaks, the St Leger, the Champion sprints, the big handicaps. The early Sussex days as grafting amateur, then professional jockey. Then the first pre-war training set-up in Yorkshire, sharing quarters with Noel Murless.

"Ryan's War" included a year in Ireland foxhunting seven days a week. "What was I doing in Ireland? Chasing deserters. Not their fault. Two of them were working for me." There were eighteen months in the Shetland Isles. "Terrible suicide rate. Boredom. But I loved it. Best salmon fishing in the world." And finally there was "how I became Monty's minder."

Normandy 1944, and the Paras had taken a pounding. "We had been decimated—decimated you understand! Only 84 of us left, and I was summoned to headquarters. Never been so frightened in my life. There was Churchill waving his arms around and saying, 'I'm giving you the most important job in the war—guarding General Montgomery's life.' We formed a ring of steel around him every night, I can tell you. Amazing man, Montgomery. Tough? Oh, yes, tough and clever, too."

After all that, no one carried his military rank more proudly than Captain Price, who returned not to some grace-and-favour mansion, but to a tiny yard at Lavant, West Sussex, with a caravan in the paddock. This was clearly a young man in a hurry. Dorothy, his calm and wryly patient wife, was met on Sunday and married on Wednesday. The winners, albeit at Newton Abbot, Haldon and Buckfastleigh, began to flow. The peerless Fred Winter became the jockey. The sky became the limit. Ryan's assistant and amateur rider for many years was Bob McCreery, now a highly successful breeder and the owner of Busaco, the big winner at Goodwood on Friday. "There were two things about Ryan," says McCreery. "First that he had that remarkable gift, understanding for hoses. Second that he was prepared to work fearlessly to test fresh ideas. The result was that when he said they were really right they always won."

Allowing for as much hindsight as you like, McCreery's analysis spotlights a quality raised again and again by other close observers as Ryan progressed through the Schweppes Hurdle era, when Josh Gifford was his brilliant young jockey, and then on to the Flat and Tony Murray's two classic successes on Ginevra and Bruni. That quality is the trainer's equivalent of the fairy wand.

Start to discuss this sort of area, and you are usually joined only by sceptics or fools, the present British training system being more geared for keeping a horse on the boil for whatever suitable targets may crop up. The art of preparing a horse for one precise peak is often ignored in a sea of pressure and statistics. "Of course it's nothing to do with charts and blood counts," says Ryan flamboyantly. "It's what a horse says to me in its work, and in the box, that really counts."

As he turns and thunders off over the horizon on a racing four-year-old, hardly the usual hack for a septuagenarian, there's time to ponder the parting shot: "I have one final throw. That black horse, Spin of a Coin. A charmer. An athlete. I'm going to take him to Tokyo to run in the Japan Cup on 27 November. Might bloody win it, too. Be fun, fun, what?"

Land of the Rising Sun, you have had your warning.

The Captain didn't get to Tokyo. Lucky for the Japanese perhaps but our game and its headlines seem a bit empty without him. Not that there would have been much room sixteen months later when the Boxing Day results looked like a case for the Monopolies Commission.

Boxing Day Blitz
January 2nd 1983

It had been the greatest training performance since they first tamed *equus Caballus* and, seasonally enough, part of its secret was revealed the morning after. It was Tuesday, and 21 horses who 24 hours earlier had been the largest and most successful task force ever in action on a single racing day were trotting round Michael Dickinson's Yorkshire paddock, every one of them as sound as the bell on the Harewood skyline.

"That really put the cap on it," said the 33-year-old Dickinson as he looked back on Boxing Day's world-record twelve victories. (Not to mention five seconds, two thirds, a fourth and one miserable seventh.) "Look at any trainer who had even three runners the day before and I will guarantee at least one of them will be stiff and sore. I have always said that keeping them sound was the most difficult thing with jumpers, and to have all twenty-one okay was just unbelievable."

This concentration on the day after and the day ahead, rather than the much-acclaimed moments of triumph, is typical of the tall, stork-like ex-jockey who in just two full seasons as trainer is making racing statisticians as rewrite-conscious as Soviet historians. "It's ridiculous," said Peter Jones, whose publication *Trainers' Record* has become an indispensable computer-based stable analysis. "Everyone else would be happy with a ratio of twenty-per-cent winners to runners. Last year, Michael's figures were well over forty-per-cent, and with

52 winners from 102 starters this season, his present rate is some fifty-per-cent. Amazing." And that does not include yesterday's racing.

But these superlatives should not divert attention from the infinite capacity to take pains. Every one of Dickinson's fifty horses was out at exercise on Christmas Sunday, and their longest day began well before the dawn had crept in from the East Riding.

In best commando style, Dickinson himself took on the day's longest journey, the 400-mile round trip to Kempton, although he usually prefers to stay behind with his horses rather than sample the delights (and diversions) of the race-course. "That's on normal days," said Michael. "But this was special, and anyway we like always to have someone at each course to saddle and supervise. Normally it's either Mum or Dad, but on Monday everyone was busy. Mum went to Wetherby (twenty miles round trip), Dad to Sedgefield (120 miles), Alan Webster was at Market Rasen (120 miles) and Michael Stoute's travelling lad, Vincect Kelly, did things at Huntingdon (200 miles).

The mention of the parents reminds us about mother Monica, as cool and calculating now as in her brilliant riding days, and father Tony, the picker of the horses and the wisest bird in the racing jungle. They went training when Michael got keen, and the boy rode 378 winners in eleven seasons, despite being so tall that the great teacher, "Frenchie" Nicholson, at first said: "Stick to window cleaning." Tony's abdication after thirteen years and more than five hundred winners didn't change the family style of the whole operation, and such insistence on home-grown riding talent that nine of Monday's 12 winners were ridden by five different Dickinson jockeys. Those are all impressive ingredients, but Michael Dickinson himself remains the master chef.

He's a rare blend all right, totally obsessive but rigidly undogmatic: "All my plans were made over a week before but I would hate to think that they couldn't change." Impressively confident but supremely self questioning: "It was very good to have the first and third in the King George, but to be quite honest both horses ran moderately. Silver Buck wasn't fit enough, and Wayward Lad hadn't got over his race at Cheltenham, ran a stone below his form with Fifty Dollars More. I don't blame myself for how they were, but I do for not appreciating beforehand. And I'm no judge of a good thing. If you had made me put a million pounds on just one horse, it would have been The Welder . . . and he got beat."

Two lemonades in celebration, and then the devoted Joan had driven him the long trek back to Harewood before a full team debriefing explained just how Dickinson had put himself into *The Guinness Book of Records*. Down in Melbourne the previous holder, Colin Hayes, chewed on such faraway names as Sedgefield and Market Rasen, and wondered how the Dickinson dozen compared with the Hayes ten-hander last January in Adelaide and at Caulfield, Victoria. "I don't know much about your jumping," said Hayes, "but I guess to saddle twelve must be something special in any language." Hold the page, McWhirter, there may be plenty more to come.

*Michael Dickinson,
the most successful
jumping trainer of all
time, still can't believe
it (Chris Smith)*

The Guinness Book of Records *took quite a pounding in
the next few months, Dickinson ending the 1982/83 season
with records in prize money (£350,000) and in races won
(127), besides breaking the bank with the first five home in
the Cheltenham Gold Cup. It was Michael's year all right.
But down in the bargain basement end of the store another
little tale was unwinding. This trainer was no mug either.*

Queen of the Bargain Chasers
January 9th 1983

The lady and her latest tramp. The worst horse in Britain jumps the lowest fence
at the slowest speed. With anyone else, that would be the end of things. But this is
Dina Smith, and on present form you couldn't let her in a piggery for fear of half
the porkers getting airborne.

The horse is Ragflint, a four-year-old whose limited flat-race career showed
such spectacular lack of promise that the 450 guineas Dina paid for him in
December would have been much less but for competition from the hamburger
trade. Yet Dina liked him, and while others wanted to laugh at her, they
remembered all too clearly what happened when they last performed.

In National Hunt racing there is no keener competition than the search for the winner of the Daily Express Triumph Hurdle, the four-year-old championship run at Cheltenham every March. Since this is that generation's first permitted jumping season, the flat-racing scene is combed for likely talent, and sums of ten, twenty and even fifty thousand pounds are shelled out to win the cherished prize. Imagine, then, the consternation among the pillars of the profession last spring when victory went to this smiling, unpretentious little 35-year-old woman from Eastergate in Sussex with Shiny Copper, an ex-French reject costing less than three thousand guineas. Worse, she had run three other bargain-offer horses—a quarter of her entire string in only her third public training season—and they had finished fifth, seventh and tenth in the mammoth 29-strong field.

That was last year, but it's been happening again. Last Monday at Cheltenham we had an important Triumph Hurdle trial, and just as Fred Winter's expensive and impressive Wollow Will looked like winning, one of Dina's horses came roaring up the outside. It was called Cut A Dash, and had been bought for the princely sum of 2,300 guineas from the Royal trainer, Dick Hern, after Willie Carson had delivered the three-word verdict: "He can't gallop."

"Well, it wasn't their Flat form that attracted me to them," said Dina, with that lovely ingenuous brown-eyed smile. And, as you look around her ramshackle little establishment hard by Fontwell racecourse, you have also to conclude that it's not for sweeping lawns and handsome stable blocks that Dina's owners rightly consider themselves the luckiest in the land. For in truth "Eastmere Stables", with its fourteen higgledy-piggledy boxes, its cobwebby corrugated-iron roofs and its wheel-less caravan, which is home and office for Dina and her husband, Al, looks as if even a kid-brother cyclone could shift it at a single puff.

What's more, the ever-busy A27 to the north means that all access to Goodwood Forest and to John Dunlop's generously available gallops and advice has to be had by horse-box, and that means cramming four animals into a battered H-registration Bedford.

But then you see the horses. For whatever their surroundings, these brutes look a million dollars. Their coats gleam, eyes shine, muscles ripple, and that sort of condition needs more explaining than the simple story of horse-mad girl and devoted husband giving up everything to look after a couple of giveaway horses (Dina herself rode the first and appropriately named winner, Strong Love), and then only going public when one of the horses was sold and the new owner didn't want it moved.

The solution lies in the style of Dina as she moves around her horses. She reminds you of some gifted, ruddy-faced nurse, full of chat and love and charm, but tough enough to snuff out any trouble on the ward.

Now she walks behind her latest purchase, a tiny, eight-stone cameo of the farmer and the plough-horse. "I like to let them do things slowly, hop over poles like this, get themselves together. Then maybe they can blossom," she says sympathetically.

Sister will soon have to move herself and her patients to a bigger, more organised hospital. There's talk of Ogbourne and Lingfield. The racing world will look on with affection and almost disbelief. For if talent is like a torch, this lady surely has the lamp.

Even Dina couldn't make Ragflint a winner but she continued on her talented way and also produced a baby daughter, Jean, who is now yet another family member in the winner's enclosure. When 1983's flat racing started, an equally unlikely stable put its flag atop the mast. It's a long way to Lancashire, but it was worth the trip.

The House that Jack Built
May 8th 1983

You could hire the cages for sixpence each. The butcher's son, a little cheeky-faced black-haired ten-year-old would take a row of three. "Then if a man came along with three rabbits for, say, five shillings, I would promise to pay later, put them in my cages and sell at a profit. That's me, you've got to be quick to survive." The kid in Leeds market was 35 years ago. Jack Berry was on his way.

With those gifts there must have been an easy route, through the stalls, shops and showroom to slinky suits, big cars and gold bracelets before he was thirty.

But the ragamuffin who used to walk the four miles to Temple Newson every weekend with his sister to scrabble for coal in the pit heat, wanted, of all things, to be either a jump jockey or a bull fighter. The horses won, and while Jack Berry, now a trainer, today heads the winner's list for the flat-racing season, his position there and the Mercedes by the gate have been gained only by more work, more worries and more back-breaking injuries than you would get in a thousand corridas.

There is even a more immediate threat. One of his seventeen winners had shown positive to a routine post-race dope test and fuelled the usual jealous whispers that sidle in behind any rapid racing success story. Such things don't bother Jack. "Yes there has been a positive test," he said. "It's theobromide— almost certainly from a batch of contaminated nuts. We have no secrets except sincere hard work. Anyone is welcome to come and have a look."

So on Thursday that's exactly what we did, taking the road north from Preston, turning westwards to Cockerham and then winding back from the sea to lane's end and the stamp and clatter of the stables that Jack built (his wife Jo mixed the cement) over the past eight years. This is flat, no-nonsense country with the highest winter rainfall in the land, and as Berry sorted out the eighteen horses you could have been much further than 250 miles from Newmarket's manicured lawns and four-legged million-dollar dreams.

Jack, in sharp black jodhpurs and a snappy wool helmet-cover, is riding Bri-Eden, a nine-year-old winner of sixteen sprint races and typical of the trainer's attitude to the game. "He's had everything wrong with him, but we've got him right. I love sprinters and especially two-year-olds," he says in that quick-fire Yorkshire patter. "They're my little babbies. No fancy prices mind, but if I like one at the sales I buy it. Finding an owner comes later."

Only six soggy weeks into the season, the Berrys have already run eleven of their 25 two-year-olds, only three have failed to win, and on Tuesday at York the doubly successful Oyston's Special will be bidding to establish herself as the fastest filly seen this term.

"We don't play at it," says Jack, as the little team circle the do-it-yourself yard whose fifty boxes include a set made of floorboards from a disused mill. "We get to work on the animals the moment they get back from the sales in the autumn. We bit them and lead them through the stalls. You cannot win two-year-old races if your horses aren't a hundred per cent at jumping out of the stalls. And if you want to get them ready you have got to graft. We were working our horses when the other stables were all having their Christmas dinner."

Not surprisingly from a Yorkshireman who aims to bring Lancashire its first top-class flat-racing stable, there are other, even more caustic comments about the better-breeched southern yards, some of which charge as much as £50 more than Berry's £77-a-week training fees. "Many of them have all their facilities on tap. We have had to provide everything—stables, indoor school, horse walker, starting stalls, all-weather gallop . . . the lot.

Jack Berry with the fruits of his Herculean labours, May 1983 (Chris Smith)

"We feed the horses just as well, so why should other yards charge so much more? And I think it is diabolical that some of them said that they couldn't afford the last pay increase to £81 a week for stable lads. My lads were getting £84 before the increase. If you pay them peanuts, of course you will only get monkeys."

All good challenging stuff, and certainly the collective "we" is as real here as anywhere in the racing game. The whole yard join Jack, Jo and their two sons for breakfast along the eighteen foot long kitchen table like some leather-legged ship's crew between watches. "I am certain that this has to be a team effort," says Jack. "I used to think I was God's gift. I would do the riding, drive the box, plait the manes, everything. Now, with Jimmy Thompson, Neville Hill and the rest of the staff so good, I have to delegate to let them breathe. They have won 46 out of 51 awards for 'best turned-out horse'—they must be doing more than putting the tack on."

Such Olympian detachment rings oddly from a man so espoused to the work ethic as a battling freelance jump jockey that he now looks brighter and younger than when we rode together in the mid-sixties. In those days he even kept the cupboard open during one freeze-up by mucking out 7,000 pigs near Huddersfield, and when he first started training as well as riding at Doncaster in 1969 things were so tight that little Alan would get the breakfast ready for his dad to snatch between lots, and he was all of five years old.

But as in those old market days the drive is in the mind as well as the muscles. It was during three months' vertebrae-broken immobilisation in Lincoln Hospital that Jack sketched out the plans of his future yard, and even now he frequently wakes up in the middle of the night, makes a cup of tea and then charts his horses' prospects. "Alone in the middle of the night plotting ahead. Super."

William Blake would have recognised it: "Energy is the only life. . . ."

Jack Berry's great run slowed down a bit later in the season but he still collected 48 races and attracted so many owners that he started 1984 with over seventy horses in training. Jack has been challenging life all his days. Here's another gauntlet thrown down rather further afield. In fact, although the trainer is based in Ireland, we had to travel to the other end of the earth to hear the story. It was no great hardship.

Walking it in Tokyo
December 4th 1983

When Stanerra won the Japan Cup last Sunday, she didn't just collect sixty-five million yen in prize money, she threatened some of the most stoutly held beliefs in the game.

The first is that no one could ever stage a true world championship. For, as Stanerra flashed over the Tokyo finishing line, her four closest pursuers (all within a length of her) came from Japan, France, America and New Zealand, a race-finish had involved horses from the Northern and Southern Hemispheres, as well as from East and West.

Not all of those animals were super-champions in their own land, but the result shows that a real international showdown is entirely viable granted the will to compete. It also refutes the previously accepted wisdom that Japan's best horses were still some distance from the world stage. For their Kyoei Promise was only beaten a head by Stanerra, and must be considered unlucky, as he broke down so badly that it needed the accident van to get him off the track.

Indeed, the Japanese attitude at the press conference before and after the race was a revelation. In the previous two Japan Cups, the locals have not been nearer than fifth, and in this year's pre-race briefing they looked about as optimistic as cattle in a canning factory. Afterwards, the massed ranks of Nipponese scribblers stomped and whistled with delight as jockey Shebata and trainer Takamatsu took the first of a thousand bows, and then astounded us excuse-prone Westerners with the comment: "No complaints—the best horse won."

But if that was a lesson in modesty, the biggest challenge of the event was in the training methods adopted for the winner. A challenge locally because they once again contrasted sharply with the impersonal and over-regimented Japanese system, and a gauntlet down internationally because this is the first world-class race to be won by methods which owe as much to applied aerobics as they do to equestrian tradition.

Stanerra's trainer, Frank Dunne only took out a licence last year, and he combines training with a heavy business schedule as managing director of Dunne's Stores, the largest supermarket chain in Ireland. All these pressures can give him a slightly sad hound-dog look rather older than his forty years, but there is no tentativeness as he says: "After Stanerra finished fourth in last year's Japan Cup, I said that I would come back and win it this time because I was going to improve her ten pounds. My whole philosophy was that aerobics applied to commonsense and general horsemanship can dramatically improve a horse's cardio-viscular capability, and therefore its performance."

When a new trainer, particularly a rich one with only fourteen head on his books, starts giving you that heavy stuff, you don't have to be a total cynic to remember such old chestnuts as "good horses train themselves," and "a stable is only as good as its staff." But while it's true that the devotion in Tokyo of Christy Ryan, and of Walter and Michael Swinburn, had to be seen to be believed, the strength and originality of Dunne's control had become clear long before he got stuck next to me on the long haul home on Thursday-Friday night.

For instance, it was Frank Dunne who insisted, albeit by telephone, that the treatment for the set-fast (a back-spasm) and blood disorder that bedevilled Stanerra after her 35-hour marathon from her Sandown Park stop-over to Shiroi quarantine centre, should be to walk the big mare all hours of the day and night. She and her increasingly footsore attendants became the feature of the international barn as they trudged round for hour after hour. It was Dunne who six weeks ago prescribed a routine of twenty miles' worth of steady exercise a day to get Stanerra back to her racing weight of 520 kilogrammes (over half a ton) after a coughing lay-off had seen as much as 536kg on the scale. (She was still the heaviest horse in the sixteen-runner field on Sunday—a full 100kg more than the little English challenger, High Hawk.)

And it was Dunne who, with the endless night from Bahrain to Rome beneath us, gave out the biggest challenge to his sport on Friday. After describing his belief in aerobic routines of speed-clocked mile work-outs with five-minute intervals, the importance of heart recovery rates as a test of fitness, of oxygen debt, glycogen loading, blood counts and long hours of exercise, he said quietly, more professor than protagonist: "We are eight generations of horses into this century, and have vastly increased veterinary knowledge, and yet have not significantly improved the performance of the thoroughbred. I refuse to believe it is impossible."

A year ago, Michael Dickinson started, but soon abandoned, an experiment with intervals training. He was over to see Frank Dunne last month, and you can be sure last Sunday's success didn't go unheeded. After Stanerra in Japan, other things may change. For the better.

5.The Punters

*If money is the root of all evil, it's not odd that racing
has its fair share of villainy. What is surprising to this
observer is that the share isn't any larger. When you
think that thousands, and in some cases literally millions,
of pounds are at stake on something as unpredictable as a
horse race, it is nothing short of amazing that more
people don't try and bend that unpredictability into an art
form.*

*The main defence has always been that racing, in whatever
country, is never a very large family. Big hoods may come
and go but they have to compete against other predators
who won't allow too many strokes to be pulled against
them. They know the game too well. Maybe even like it too
much.*

*Here is a selection of pieces where the money factor has
taken people different ways. Some clever, some criminal,
some far-sighted and some, dare we say it, even a bit
of fun.*

*The first is criminal. A French hurdle race so bent that it
would make a corkscrew blush. What made it worse for me
is that, from an earlier life, I knew most of the jockeys
personally. They were anything but hardened crooks, but
over a period rot began to set into the apple store and by the
time the big, almost absurd, stroke of pulling half the field
in a major race was tried, most people had forgotten what
clean fruit was really like.*

*The affair was a lesson to us all. The race was called the
Prix Bride Abattue.*

The French Misconnection
January 12th 1975

Could it happen here? That was the question we have had to ask during the past
week, with French racing convulsed by the long-dreaded eruption of the Prix
Bride Abattue affair.

On Monday the scandal over this allegedly "fixed" Auteuil hurdle race was
given a macabre first anniversary with the arrest of the 1973 champion jump
jockey, 24-year-old Pierre Costes, charged with pulling his horse, the favourite in
the disputed race. Ironically Bride Abattue means "flat out" (literally, "bridle
loosed"), which is exactly the reverse of what happened to the favourites.

After Costes, three other well-known jump jockeys went "inside"—Jean-Paul

*Overleaf: Betting on
the Epsom Downs
(Chris Smith)*

Ciravagena, thirty, winner of the Grand Steeplechase de Paris on Morgex in 1972, Jean-Pierre Renard, thirty-one, winner of France's jumping classic this year, and Jean-Pierre Philipperon, thirty, the gifted elder brother of the flat-race jockey, Maurice Philipperon.

Two other jockeys were held overnight then released, but for another less-known rider, Christian da Meda, and a trainer, Jacques Beaume, were held and charged. Then investigating judge Michaud had the police swoop on nine gamblers in Marseilles and Toulon, and so the teeth of this Mafia-like fixing organisation were beginning to show. For besides the death threats, extortion and thuggery that earlier put jockey Luriou, suspected as the Mafia's go-between, behind bars, there have been one jockey's suicide two years ago, and three other violent deaths more recently—all reckoned to be the result of the gang's machinations.

The whole thing makes Dick Francis read like Galsworthy, but quite apart from the other arrests, just imagine that Ron Barry, Jeff King, Pat Buckley and Johnny Haine were all *enfermé* (in jail). Worse, since the Prix Bride Abattue was the selected race for the Tierce, the French 1-2-3 pool bet which now has seven million players and £8 million in the take every weekend. Fixing that was akin to arranging four First Division draws on the coupon.

The racing heart of the affair is Maisons-Laffitte, a leafy chateau-dominated Parisian suburb just ten miles west of the Arc de Triomphe. It is also France's biggest jump-training centre, and all seven accused work there. It's rather like having Lambourn and more in Richmond Park, and this is one detail of the case from which Britain can claim to be free of reasonable comparison. So grouped, and so close to the capital, Maisons-Laffitte has worked as a greenhouse to ripen this rotten fruit.

There are two other big differences between France and Britain in all this. The first is that the Prix Bride Abattue operation could only work with a gigantic pool on a single race, the idea being that they squared the jockeys on the better-fancied horses so as to make for a long-priced pay-out.

In fact, the number of combinations of all the other nine runners triggered the off-course Paris Mutuel alarm system, and suspicions were almost laughably confirmed when the race soon split into two well-divided groups, the nine unsquared runners at the front, the 15 others at some distance. The pay-out, which was frozen, was £478,000—odds of 4,489–1 for the first three in correct order, and 785–1 for the first three in any order. Yet to make sure of the combination, the input would still have to be so big that in Britain, with nothing like an £8 million pool, the operation would drastically reduce its own effectiveness. And although attempts have been made to rig the Tote 1–2 forecast, the possibilities of the really long-priced pay-off don't compare, either.

Secondly, no one should under-estimate the poacher-turned-gamekeeper role of the bookmakers over here, whose conduct over the Gay Future Bank Holiday coup shows that they have not lost their ability to scent chicanery.

The third big difference is the money and lifestyle in France. Racing gets five per cent of the thirty per cent the government takes from the Tierce. The winner of a "seller" at Auteuil receives more than Comedy of Errors got for beating Lanzarote at Cheltenham last weekend. Parisian jump racing takes place four days a week on tracks within an hour's drive.

By British standards, the leading French jump jockeys are affluent and idle, but then life is still short, taxes are high and the falls crumplingly hard. What are the temptations of the big tax-free take arranged over those endless games of poker? In Costes's case, it is claimed that he needed to settle some of the debts incurred at the table.

I understand that our own security services are especially concerned about the troubles of desperate, rather than greedy, eyes over here looking to a "bent" race as a way of getting some tax-free loot. It is also dangerous to assume that human nature is any different across the Channel, whether it concerns the jockeys, or stewards, led bravely by M. des Poncins, grasping the nettle as a cleansing towel for all the public's mistrust.

The whole business is out in the steamy exposure of the front pages now, but at Maisons-Laffitte on Friday, eating at Le Tastevin Fontaine, you had to realise that it was a family tragedy. I met old friends from riding days at Sagnes, Pau and Auteuil, and then, scanning photos of the wall, I remembered with a jolt that some of them would now have only the walls of a cell to look at.

I remembered being offered £500 to "stop" a horse—just a veiled suggestion, but it was there all right. The horse didn't win, but only because it couldn't go in the mud. I hadn't any great debts at the time, and I didn't fancy the involvement. In other situations, the pressures and temptations might have had a different result. Anyone who doubts where such pressures can lead ought to go to France, where the sinners are come like Dr Faustus to judgment.

Meanwhile the hunt for a big chief, the brains behind the operation, goes on. There is a possibility that he may even be a now-exiled, but once-notorious, member of the racing underworld in this country. Whoever he is, with racing needing credibility like a tent needs poles, we have to prevent the setting up of a nursery ground for his choking seeds over here—even if sometimes that means being cruel to be kind.

If late nights, easy money and fairy stories are the jockeys' forbidden fruit, they would also be fatal for our next heroes: the early morning experts whose after-dawn judgements can save you countless cash when tales of great gallops are put around the race-track. But a visit to Newmarket showed that nowadays we are talking about a dying art.

Arty Edwards—King of Touts
April 1976

The watery eyes that have watched more gallops than Hugh Hefner's have watched Bunny-tails, came down from the enormous pair of 11 × 80s and gave us our cautionary thought for the week: "A horse is like a woman. You are attracted to her, but you don't know what you've got until you have put a lot along the line."

The speaker was 71-year-old Arty Edwards, the most senior and most forth-right of the Newmarket touts (or work-watchers as some rodent operators call them), and the name behind *The Times*'s ultra-discreet title, Our Newmarket Correspondent. Arty's caution is worth pondering this week when, only a few days after Red Rum's heroic pursuit of Rag Trade's hairy heels, we have all been around the three-year-old classic trials stoking up enough fleeting impressions and unimpeachable rumours to make even a lobby correspondent choke.

"In the old days," says Arty, with the nostalgia of one who backed five Derby winners at 100–1 before anyone else realised their ability, "horses were really galloped. Trainers would get them to the races 95 per cent fit. Now they get them eighty per cent, and just hope for the best.

Whether or not you share Arty's admiration for the old methods, there is no doubt that the present-day system makes his job, and mine, more difficult. How fit was Malinowski at Newmarket last week? Were his opponents Oats, and in particular Whistlefield, both less galloped? How far advanced were the French stars, Manado and Flying Water?

In America, with its track training system, we could have known the exact interval times of all their latest gallops. In dog racing we would even know their weight. But all Arty needed was for them to work regularly and hard across Newmarket Heath, and he would have told you their fitness to the ounce.

"Gallops!" he snorted, looking out across the deserted green carpet of the famous lime kilns last Thursday morning. "You hardly see any real gallops nowadays—maybe eight or nine of a morning. I remember when we had six hundred up here, and coming so fast that George could hardly have time to look up from recording their names."

George Robinson is the other half of the team—Arty's brother-in-law and, like him, equipped with binoculars and an indexed book of every horse in Newmarket (more than 1,300), with coded hieroglyphics for identifying marks, which they painstakingly fill in over the winter months. Two horses come into view over half a mile away. The big glasses go up, and the voice mutters: "Two of Robert Armstrong's—Ahdeek and that hurdler Priestlaw." It is an extraordin-ary encyclopaedic skill, but sadly a dying art, as Arty explains: "There's only Harry Baldwin (of the Press Association and *Sporting Chronicle*) and us now. There used to be eight or nine," says Arty, "but then who can blame them? There's nothing to watch. Look at that horse—only cantering."

But however strong his hankering for the hard graft of the past, there is still no doubting Arty's eye for the present. He tipped Bolkonski to beat Grundy in last year's Two Thousand Guineas, and last week was correctly insistent that Charley's Revenge was the only Newmarket two-year-old ready to win. As *The Times* racing correspondent, Michael Phillips, says: "He is extraordinarily well-informed, and it's all his own judgment—not just rumours and stable talk."

Perhaps what he misses most is the running battle between trainers and touts of the past. "That Major Beatty, he was one of the worst. One day he saw that little Chippy Jackson was watching him secretly gallop some two-year-olds in the afternoon. He rode up nice as pie and said: "Afternoon, Jackson, can I have a look at your binoculars?" Then he whipped off and watched the whole gallop through them, and poor little Chippy never saw a thing. I don't think he ever forgave the Major."

Sadly Arty Edwards went to the great training ground in the sky three years after that story was written and so his brother-in-law George Robinson continues the early morning vigil as almost the last in the line. But while George and Arty deal only in what they see, others of us are more fallible to the fancy line. When it comes to punting, the reliable guide isn't just a system, it's the holy grail. Or it would be if it worked.

A Gallery of Dreams
September 1980

The trail led from an art gallery on Wimbledon Common to the Ayr Gold Cup and a 33–1 bet called Gambler's Dream. It had to be too good to be true.

There are horses as well as wombles on Wimbledon Common, but any racing connections are confined to the past. The Annexe Gallery, which looks out across the pond, pays no attention as they clop by, and has no equestrian works on its walls, yet if you delve into the cubby-hole at the back you will find endless lists and charts of every race and racehorse in Britain.

It can be explained, if you have got three-and-a-half hours and an IQ of about 250, by listening to the owner of the gallery, a tall, bespectacled ex-scholar, barrister, management consultant and *Private Eye* pillar named Christopher Hull. The talk can flit from Verdi to Priestley, from painting to politics, but when you get it back to the ledger, letters, statistics and facts of his racing interest, the awful truth emerges that this bystander is claiming that most devastating of achievements, a system that works.

Now, to any of us who have been on the betting rocks, this is the sort of siren call that makes you clamp your hands over your ears. But Hull has the engaging arrogance of the brilliant man ("I always knew I could be top of the class") and a devilishly straightforward plan. "All other analysts, even the great Phil Bull of Timeform, include some opinion in their calculations," says Hull. "I deal only in facts, in the exact measurement of form."

A computer was originally programmed to collect the endless statistics, hence the name Computerform, under which Hull has traded since 1965 to an exclusive 300 subscribers who, if they followed the instructions exactly, could have a tax-paid profit of 22 per cent a year, the selections being right no less than 47 per cent of the time. Admittedly, there were some caveats like: "Only eighty 'strong' bets a year." And some mumbo jumbo about "Double" and "Pure Double Top", but in principle you could get a Computerform rating on every horse in every race. What better panacea to have on call for Scotland's riskiest four days of the year, the Western Meeting starting at Ayr last Wednesday?

Needless to say, by Friday morning we were in need of all the help we could get. The Gulf Stream had brought in a storm that had turned Ayr racecourse into a tropical swamp. Old Sea Pigeon had made his 91st comeback, and with the gibes of the disgruntled punters beginning to touch the nerve, it seemed time to call up Wimbledon Common and get some guidance on that appalling 24-runner cavalry charge called the Ayr Gold Cup.

Well, it has to be recorded that Hull first said that Computerform had no recommended "strong" bet all week, but with a bit of prompting he did admit that they had clearly top-rated a 33–1 outsider rejoicing in the name of Gambler's Dream.

A glance down the paper revealed the gelding to like soft going, to be owned by a London casino and to be handled by a new Epsom trainer, David Wilson, as yet without a winner but formerly a vital part of several big handicap coups with John Sutcliffe Snr. Wilson is cool and shrewd, and comes from Ayr. Computerform cautions or not, you had to admit that this looked like "the business".

Any hopes of staying sensible went within five minutes of reaching the track. Ken Gillie, William Hill's Northern man, pressed a piece of paper into my hand with the muttered assurance: "It's from a very good source." Gillie has some of the best moles in the business.

His note read: "Gambler's Dream has been the subject of a substantial gamble, including one bet of 33 monkeys." Meaning £500 at 33–1.

Privy to this sort of information, £20 each way looked like the winter holiday money in one easy sweep. All other endless tips and gossip that invariably surround an Ayr Gold Cup were immediately dropped for a lengthy interview with Gambler's Dream's apprentice rider, Billy Newnes. Carrot-haired Billy, born in Liverpool twenty years ago, is rapidly building as big a reputation for himself on the track as he first made in the stable lads' boxing ring. "He's got a great chance," he said.

There is not much left to tell except that the television commentary was laced with knowing references to Gambler's Dream. It took one minute 15.9 seconds for the winner to cover the six furlongs. Our horse was nowhere.

Long afterwards, with Wilson and Newnes's shrugged professional explanation—"never went a yard"—still burning in my pocket, and the long trek home begun, I rang the art gallery in Wimbledon to say something if only "Goodbye". Hull had gone to the opera. Some gambler. Some dream.

Despite that reverse, no doubt the hunt for the infallible system will continue its expensive old way. Anyone who has ever smelt the bonfire at the end of that road can surely warm to my next two stories. The first about a man who was surely in Damon Runyon's mind when he was giving us Harry the Horse and the rest of the gang some forty years ago.

The Dodger's Art
November 22nd 1981

Despite the rain, the knight in shiny black oilskins ducked past two scufflers at Kempton on Wednesday, leapt back on his viewing stool and, as the runners cleared the last hurdle, began jump racing's loudest victory refrain: "Come on my son—take the bunny home!" The Dodger had backed another winner.

It is now 25 years since Simon McCartney abandoned his line in sun-blind supply, and earned his nickname by "dodging" through the crowd to reach bookmakers offering odds he wanted. Over that time, the Dodger has become unique among professional punters, a survivor, a success and, more than that, a friend of the family.

This is normally a "wide boy" game and, with his broad shoulders, undertaker's overcoat (on dry days), fashion hair-cut and crumpled, lived-in face, the Dodger's looks don't belie the assumption any more than his fractured London vowels sound different from some barrow boy who has got ahead. But this is no pedlar of cheap conspiracies: "Of course there are some people who stop and start, but I don't back their horses. This game is 95 per cent straight, and I don't listen to fairy stories."

"The 'game' he is referring to is National Hunt racing, which became his passion from the age of sixteen, even though his only connection was a keen-betting lorry-driver father: "Flat racing has never done anything for me. I only went once last year. It all happens too quick. In this game you get to know the horses, watch them going round for years and form your own opinion."

More than a thousand miles a week are driven in the low-slung Lancia two-seater from his unlikely country base way out near Cardiff (for some obscure reason there is also a black London taxi in the stable), and long hours are spent relentlessly combing through results. "There are only two places to study form," says the Dodger, who still claims to be the romantic side of fifty. "In the car park before racing, or in bed." He adds, almost straight-faced: "You can spread the books out all around you."

However it's done, there is no doubt that Mr McCartney is formidably well-informed, and it has long been his boast that he doesn't ask jockeys what chance they have got—he tells them, and even sometimes "psychs" them into winning. Many years ago, in my riding days, I can remember the big, deep-coated, dark-glassed figure dropping into step on the walk into Fontwell or wherever, and starting: "Now listen, you've got a great chance here . . ." And there he was again as Grand Hussar slogged through the rain on Wednesday: "I told that Richard Linley he would win."

But it is one thing to pick winners, quite another to get your money on at decent odds. A couple of days following in McCartney's swashbuckling wake is a master class in assessing the market. "Even if I fancy a horse a lot, I won't play if I think his odds are too short," he said, striding around the betting ring's Runyonesque ebbs and flows on Thursday. "That's why I only had three bets (two losers) yesterday, but today we might have a chance."

Of course this was just one day's skirmish in the year-long campaign against the bookmakers, but I have to report that he found a price about all three of his day's fancies. All of them won, there was a pay-out of over £2,000 and as he swept off to the bar even John Banks, no blushing violet himself, was heard to mutter, "That Dodger is some character."

Naturally, this was all much too good to be true. Hadn't McCartney himself admitted to just enduring a 10-day losing run? Didn't he once go back to selling sun-blinds part-time? So when he started up about, "Seen the Ascot card tomorrow? It's a lie-down," this experienced observer congratulated himself, and quit while he was ahead. Well, you can guess what happened. Our little circus duly moved on to Ascot, and for race after race the royal heath rang to "Take the bunny away!" and other assorted cockney bellows of the Dodger in form. Good fun for spectators, and maybe for Battersea Dogs' Home, where McCartney is apt to adopt a pooch after a winning day, but pretty sick-making for those of us who didn't play.

Afterwards, flushed with triumph as if he had ridden all six winners himself (perhaps in a way he had), he taunted us over the champagne: "This could be our year. The bookmakers, in the south at least, are having to give value, and I think it's the punters' turn. Not in the betting shops—that ten per cent tax is just thievin' impossible—but out on the tracks we can win the war."

Whisper it softly, bookies beware.

*Maybe it's the risks the horses and riders are taking with
our money, perhaps it's just the usual bad weather, but
punting on jump racing has something of a battleground*

feel about it. That's why it's so good when you get it right.
Here's a story from just about the worst day of the winter
1982. Worst for whom?

Chester Barnes Serves an Ace
February 21st 1982

As little fish go, the victory of Millfield Royal in Tuesday's Hound Tor Opportunity Novices' Selling Hurdle at Newton Abbot in deepest boggiest Devon was about the smallest sprat in the racing sea. But an examination of Mr Chester Barnes's bulging back pocket afterwards would have given at least 5,400 reasons for thinking that this was also one of the sweetest strokes of the season.

For when he is not giving exhibitions of the table-tennis prowess that brought him international honours in the Sixties and Seventies, Chester Barnes is a serious gambler with a particular penchant for the horses of his friend Martin Pipe, trainer of Millfield Royal. Among their notable strikes have been Carrie Ann, backed at 33–1 to beat 22 others at Haydock in 1980, and Baron Blakeney, on whom Barnes plunged at 100–1 to win last season's Triumph Hurdle at Cheltenham. Tuesday's nine-race all-novice card hardly touched those giddy heights, but Chester was just as confident.

If he had told you beforehand (and he wouldn't have done, even his father was "put away"), you would have got no clues from a quick perusal of the *Sporting Life*, which merely recorded Millfield Royal's three unplaced hurdle races last year, ending with an undistinguished ninth of fifteen at Perth in May. If your numbed fingers had been capable of thumbing back into last summer's flat-racing form book, you would only have seen that the five-year-old mare had also failed in seven outings on the level in 1981, and if some masochistic desire had driven you to inspect the horses in the freezing parade ring, you would only have seen a skinny little creature under the No 8 saddle cloth.

Yet there were straws even in that wind which numbed other parts besides the hands. For Millfield Royal was making her first appearance under the care of Martin Pipe, who is fast becoming to west country "sellers" what Chester was to the ping-pong table, and when the fourteen riders were listed for this sixth and cheapest race on the card, Millfield Royal's jockey was not the "unknown" S. Crooks, of the morning papers, but the top-class claiming rider, Richard Dennis.

One man with highly tuned antennae for this sort of thing is that noted Bournemouth sportsman, Alan Argeband, but after receiving a pessimistic shrug from Chester he returned to his orginal belief that the Toby Balding-trained Swift Step had only the Barnstaple mare, Shady Drive, to beat and, with his hooded hawk's eyes momentarily off the target, he missed the next two vital clues. One of owner John Urch's friends popped up to have £80 to £1,000 on "Millfield" and, more important, Chester went missing.

So as the motley band of runners filed along the bank of the swollen River Teign, and then squelched off to the start of this two-mile hurdle race, a medium-sized figure, sweatered up against the cold, pushed open the doors of Newton Abbot's betting shops and proceeded to stake no less than £500 in assorted wages on Millfield Royal. Afterwards, people in the shops would remember something familiar about that round, wind-blown face, perhaps something a bit professional about the way he moved his feet. But nobody caught on, no panic telephone calls were made to head office, no flurries back at the course to trim odds, and after showing at 10–1 and 12–1, Millfield Royal started no shorter than 9–1.

The blinkered Swift Step was even-money favourite, followed by Shady Drive, who had a brakes failure and shot into a ten-length lead. Squinting contentedly down our binoculars, everything seemed to be going to plan. But what was that going clear on the far turn? Surely she can't stay there? Oh well, it must have been a fluke. But it didn't look like a fluke as Martin Pipe greeted his lean little mare afterwards, with his sharp, smiling face giving out more than a glimpse of a fox with its kill. Worse still, Chester Barnes rolled up half an hour later and explained how "she couldn't lose".

If only our early-morning brains had put the old books in the car we could have read the form which made Barnes pick out Millfield Royal for Martin Pipe at last November's Newmarket Sales. For she had won both as a two-year-old and as a three-year-old, and last year, although unlucky, she once finished fifth in a better-class race at Newcastle when owned by a willowy pillar of the northern Press Room. "The form was there if we could just get her right," said Chester. "Martin's a marvellous trainer, and last week she worked so well against some of his other horses that I knew she couldn't get beat in a seller. The rest is history."

It takes five hours to drive home from Newton Abbot. A long time to ponder that all a racing man needs is, just once, to have tomorrow's news today. Unless, of course, you persuade Chester to tell you.

After that article was published there was some dispute as to just how much money was won by Chester Barnes and his friends. But win or lose, the story was essentially a jolly one, a tale of getting it right on the night. You can't say that about our next memory. It's about the coup that everybody had secretly feared once stallion valuations went through the multi-million dollar roof. It was when Dick Francis became fact. It was when, in February 1983, a gang drove into the Aga Khan's Ballymany Stud in Southern Ireland and stole the most valuable young stallion in Europe . . . the 1981 Derby winner Shergar.

Shergar's Last Trump
February 13th 1983

When Shergar's horse-nappers rumbled out on to the Kildare road on Tuesday night, they surely congratulated themselves on having £15 million worth of stallion in the back of the wagon. The devastating truth for them, and indeed for racing, was that all they actually had was £500 of horsemeat.

For there is no pawn shop for stallions. Shergar is worthless without his pedigree. Wonder as we might at the awesome cost of equine lovemaking (this season's 55 Shergar mates will, if in foal, have paid just under £70,000 for his ardour), the whole dizzy price spiral is based on legitimate reproduction.

There is no hope that a ransom will be paid either. To do so would put every other top stallion in danger, and since the 34 members of the Shergar syndicate all have extensive investment in the bloodstock business, it would be simply inviting trouble into their own homes. Barring some uncharacteristic aberration by the Aga Khan, no one in racing expects money to pass hands.

So why did the armed gang carry out this highly-professional abduction on Tuesday night? Thoughts of terrorist involvement or even of long-term enemies of the Aga have receded since no claims were made following the kidnap. Indeed, considering the financial and social positions of such Shergar syndicate members as Stavros Niarchos, Robert Sangster and Lord Derby, it is amazing that not one of those hoax phone calls to the merry band of media mediators in Belfast had any political content.

The conclusion at this stage has to go back to greed. When Shergar drew a record ten-lengths clear of his field in the 1981 Derby the £150,000 white-faced colt was winning a prize for the Aga that was peanuts compared to his stud valuation, which was upwards of £5 million. When, after Shergar had run away with the Irish Derby, the King George VI and the Queen Elizabeth Diamond Stakes, the Aga's decision to resist higher bids from America and syndicate Shergar for "only" £10 million in Ireland was widely applauded.

Thus Shergar and horses like last year's Derby winner, Golden Fleece, who never ran after Epsom but who holds court in Tipperary for a reputed 100,000 Irish guineas, are like hooved and tailed versions of the Koh-i-Noor Diamond. And since the Ballymany stud was known to be some way short of Fort Knox, it is hardly surprising that someone had the thought of pinching this particular living jewel.

You cannot really blame a gang of rustlers for not appreciating the machinations of the top stallion business when worthy leaders of the industry scratch their own heads in disbelief. "The whole thing has become incredible," says Peter Willett, the much-respected president of the Thoroughbred Breeders' Association.

"In 1950, Citation became the first horse to win more than a million dollars in America and he was retired to stud at a valuation of a million dollars—a one to

one ratio. Now the stud valuation is fifty or even a hundred times the winnings on the track. That cannot make sense.''

But in one sense it does. In the sweltering heat of a Kentucky afternoon last July no less than $4,250,000 (about £2.7 million) was shelled out by the Sangster syndicate for a yearling; that is an eighteen-month-old untried colt who may not be able to run a cent. The great majority of such deals do not pay off, but every time a jackpot comes up—Golden Fleece himself cost about $1 million as a yearling—more high-rollers get involved.

Horse racing has always needed big investors and the presence of the Sangster syndicate in Ireland, Niarchos in France and the huge involvement by new Arab owners, such as Prince Abdulla and the Maktoum Sheikhs from Dubai, provides the funds that keep stable lads, trainers and jockeys in business.

It just remains to be seen if the racegoer himself will see any more of the present-day champions, or whether the desire to protect the owners investment will continue to mean that Derby winners are hustled off to stud because, in the ridiculous way of things, they have become racegoers that are "too valuable to race".

Shergar is also too valuable to rot away in some distant kidnapper's barn for long, although too much may have been made of the immediate danger. Unlike

Did he have a haunted look? Shergar on his winning Derby day in 1981. The tale wasn't to have a happy ending (Chris Smith)

some stallions, he appears to have a tractable temperament. Provided he is given a reasonably large barn and plenty of hay and water, there is no reason why Shergar should go barmy. Even if he is holed up much tighter, a short incarceration would not be too terrible provided there is someone around (and Ireland is full of them) who has a feeling for horses.

But however the horse is treated, tremendous damage has already been done to the carefully built reputation of the Irish bloodstock industry, for whom Shergar's return to the county where he was born was a notable coup. What is the point of beautiful stud farms, marvellous limestone soil, understanding men and government tax concessions if horse-napping becomes a popular sport? The wagon that rumbled out on to the Kildare road could have taken more than Shergar with it.

The exact events of the Shergar kidnap may never be fully told. All sorts of imaginative theories have been put up but most of them were ruled out of court by the Aga Khan's report published early in '84 which concluded that poor old Shergar was probably dead within a week of the abduction, killed by a terrorist-linked gang anxious to raise funds, but lacking knowledge of either stallion-care or bloodstock finances.
Now to an Irishman who has been raising funds out of racing, albeit the betting ring, for as long as most of us can remember. Actually he's not that old but his cunning, like his looks, is as ageless as the fox. The news, from York in August 1983, was that the fox could be viewed away.

Heaven Can Wait
August 21st 1983

At last the head is above the parapet. Barney Curley, the Irishman who set out to be a priest and ended up as the most successful punter of recent times, has emerged from the shadows this month. But characteristically for a man whose inscrutability has become an art form, we still can't be quite sure if this new high profile is a charity bonanza or a bust.

At York races last week, Barney was being unwontedly available for interviews, and for the first time never had a serious bet. "The reason," he said in the soft, flat vowels of his native Fermanagh, "is that people won't leave me alone, they are all asking for tickets." Curley, the mysterious, monk-headed figure who used to ease out of the crowd, place a five-figure bet and melt back into anonymity, is out there flogging tickets for the biggest gamble of his life. He's raffling his home.

His thoughts would cost a pretty penny. Barney Curley at York, August 1983 (Frank Hermann)

Nothing odd about that until you appreciate that if he sells only the minimum 2,000 of the tickets at £IR200 each, the receipts will drop some million punts short of the official valuation on the thirty-room, 377-acre Middleton Park Estate, near Mullingar, Co. Westmeath.

Such a possibility doesn't deter the man who lost £150,000 on last year's Epsom Derby. "The response has been enormous," he said. "I got the house by taking a chance, and so I would like it to pass to someone who is prepared to have a go. And besides, I want to make something for the charities." Large sums have been promised to the Irish Wheelchair Association, and the local Gaelic Sports club.

At first glance, it's a story that had to break during the silly season. "Sure it would be great if Barney could get four hundred thousand for his place," one influential Irish source said on Friday. "I wouldn't pay the half for it." Yet a man as distinguished as the legendary Irish broadcaster, Michael O'Hehir, is convinced of the scheme's merits, and he said colourfully: "There's no loopholes, no catches, not even a ghost." This last perhaps surprising in the ancestral home of the Boyd Rochforts, whose former occupants included a small, determined little boy who later rode to fame on a camel as Lawrence of Arabia.

What's certain is that this won't be the last chapter in the career of one of the coolest and most original minds on the Turf. The Jesuit novices back at St Mungret's College at Limerick in the Sixties would hardly have guessed that their fellow hopeful would now be aiming to set himself up as a trainer, having progressed through the equally hazardous and not over-pious occupations of managing pop stars and backing horses. He abandoned the priesthood after an attack of tuberculosis: "I thought the Good Lord had called a halt." His Svengali period included helping Frankie McBride's tear-jerker, "Five Little Fingers," become the first Irish single in the British Top Twenty, and Barney's betting involvement has included several hits which have put him into folklore.

The most famous of these was the victory of the hurdler, Yellow Sam, at Co Meath's little Bellewstown track in June, 1975. Yellow Sam started at 20–1, because the only telephone line to the off-course betting shops was "unfortunately" engaged, so the local bookies were unaware of the thousands Curley's team were investing around the country. "We won £300,000 that day. It's the last great coup where everyone got paid," said Curley, and with his new-found tongue is prepared to be quoted on other strikes with such as Fair Rambler, I'm A Driver, and Tommy Joe.

All of these horses were originally owned by Curley himself, and so his involvement in the "finesse" of having them fit and fancied for the day when the money was down has meant something of a tight-rope walk along the rules of racing. In his coming, more public, role as a trainer, Curley claims there will be no cause for alarm. "Although," he said with that slow, cunning curl of the mouth, "I think we will have the occasional bet. I just love a punt."

When quizzed on the secrets that have set him apart from the rest of us millions of mugs, he trots out the usual old boring ingredients of hard work, observation, patience and, horror of horrors, total abstinence. But sometimes you wonder if his early training hasn't given him another edge.

Facing page: Reverent betting at the Cheltenham National Hunt Festival in March 1981 (Chris Smith)

Two years ago, one of the mares in Barney's sixty-strong bloodstock team died in childbirth. With no foster mother available, Barney bottle-fed the foal himself, but after two days the vet said the case was hopeless. Not for Barney it wasn't. He strode out into the field, knelt down on the grass and looked up into the driving rain. Today the foal is a thriving, fleet-footed three-year-old, called Answer to Prayer.

As usual the Curley prayers were answered. There was a massive public response to the lottery, a small and excited English syndicate won it, and by next spring had chosen to put the estate back on the market with an asking price of half a million pounds. But Barney's success (although he was facing some legal difficulties in June 1984) has always been based as much on instinct as on straight logical calculation. For the less racing-cute amongst us, surely there is an aid that will absorb all the information and come up with the answers. In April '84 we thought we had found it.

Megabytes in the Bedroom
April 8th 1984

In John Whitley's house the computer has a bedroom of its own. It's entitled to. It has given him a winner.

This, in the most literal of senses, is every punter's dream: off to bye-byes, happy in the thought that next door a great black 64K, 8½-megabyte monster is chewing away on yesterday's form. "It's very quiet really," says Whitley from his Halifax bunker. "But it makes a bit of a humming noise on summer nights when it's got a lot of racing to digest."

Don't get the idea that this is some late April Fool's joke. Thirty-eight-year-old Whitley and his 457-page "Computer Racing Form" (price £25 from 226 Wakefield Road, Lightcliffe, Halifax—hurry while stocks last) is the most challenging opus to enter the race-analysis scene since Phil Bull, John's bewhiskered former boss, started applying his formidable intellect under the saintly pen name of William K. Temple.

Bull went on to be the founding father of the Timeform Organisation, whose annual, *Race Horses of 1983*, remains the single most prized volume (if at £45 the most costly) of the astonishing book harvest that heralds the start of this new flat-racing season. It was ten years ago that Whitley, a Warwick University mathematics major, forsook his computer manager's job at the British Oxygen Company to join Timeform and the full-time study of the game that had come to fascinate him.

The extent to which it fascinates the rest of us earthlings could be seen from last Thursday's *Sporting Life* Weekender, whose already well-informed pages contained no fewer than fourteen advertisements offering "invaluable" guides to the Flat. Whitley's computer may be whirring away in West Riding, but Trainers Record has a twenty-megabyte number buzzing down in Dorset and Superform Computer Handicap are at it in Sussex. Obviously it wasn't only Prince Monolulu who "gotta horse".

No other sport has anything to equal this proliferation of beginning-of-term advice, and if you think of the odds stacked against our great unwashed six-million-strong army of would-be horse players at the start of the season, you might conclude that only a touch of the occult would be enough. For here comes flat racing, some 7,000 horses, 150 jockeys, 200 apprentices, none of whom by the nature of the beast we have seen since November. They are taking part in an activity of which, unlike soccer, cricket or other major sports, our mass audience has absolutely no practical experience. The "game" can take no more than a minute to run, and it is exceptionally easy to lose large amounts of money on it.

The fact that large amounts of money can also, very occasionally, be won, is reason enough for many of our snouts to snuffle towards the betting shop. Another is the endless stream of statistics that racing dangles in front of its followers day by day—almost 3,000 separate events, more than 30,000 individual performances, between now and flat racing's close on 10 November. It's amazing that Bill Frindall hasn't yet donned trilby and binoculars and abandoned his famous cricket scoring sheets for the specially marked racecard. And it's no surprise that a mathematics freak like John Whitley became so hooked on feeding the computer that he actually got to the races only once last year.

"When I began to study form," said Whitley on Friday, "I could see that many of its conclusions, and particularly its handicapping, were very unscientific. My challenge was to write a programme to include all the facts, and the real satisfaction is to have been the first anywhere in the world to achieve that."

The book is certainly a monument to Whitley's diligence (the wretched machine takes about two hours to digest just one race meeting). It contains a numerate analysis of every run by every horse last year, and a comprehensive trainers' and jockeys' survey. And even if the conclusion that in terms of "performance" such talents as Pat Eddery and Greville Starkey were only 14th and 27th best in 1983 has caused a few hoots of derision, the whole thing is obviously one for the connoisseurs.

All right, so where's the winners' print-out? Well, it's not quite as easy as that. For while Whitley claims that with his ratings it's possible to win well in excess of ten per cent of better turnover, the punter has to make a whole series of calculations himself. As *The Sunday Times* bearded guru, Marten Julian, says: "It's very good, but I still believe the racecourse impression is important. That's why I think John Sharratt and his team on Raceform Notebook are so good. They watch every race every day, and record their own interpretations without fear or favour. I think you can learn a lot, and make some money from what they say."

Sharratt, greying, bespectacled and 35 years in the job, lowers the old 7 × 50s and says: "There may be all sorts of improvements in form collection, but it takes a long time to learn to 'read' a race properly, and I think the tried and trusted methods have stood the test of time."

Yet in some ways Sharratt and Whitley aren't far apart. Neither now "has the time" to bet. Something says that the computer hasn't quite cracked it yet.

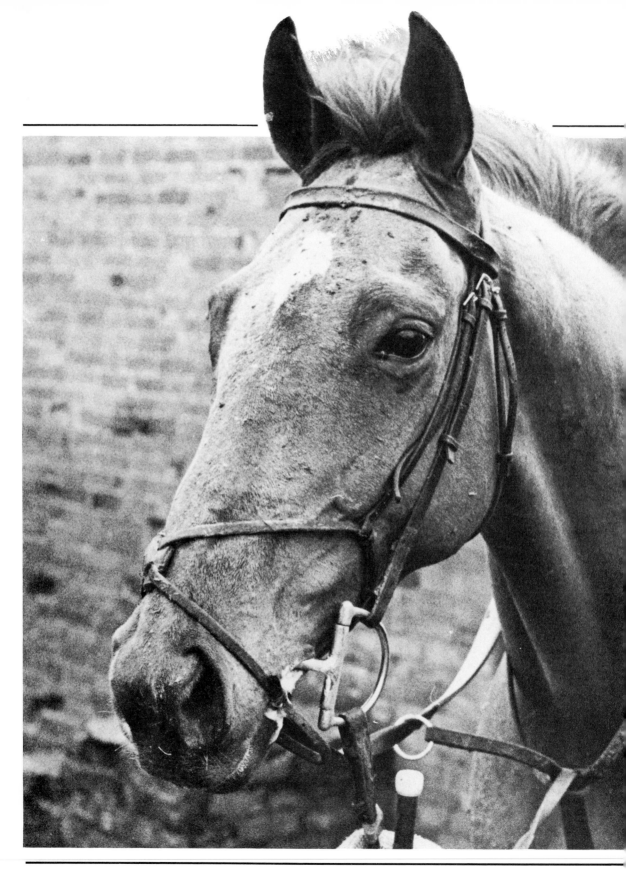

6. Personal Asides

Forgive the self-indulgence in the title, but these issues were all ones that I felt strongly about at the time and, reading the pieces again, still do now. They are just my witness to the fact that it is not only a famous Sunday newspaper that can boast "all of human life is there". We start with a train trip and it still seems a swindle that we never got sponsored by British Rail.

Not such Strangers on a Train
December 1974

It might be going a bit far to say that you have never lived until you have been on a race train. But you will certainly have missed an experience. Mind you, on Thursday we also missed the train. That is, we missed the 10 am from Charing Cross to Folkestone races, which is the really hardened *cognoscenti*'s choice. Yet there was still plenty of human flavour on the 11 o'clock, with a cast list nearly as strong as that for *Murder on the Orient Express*, even if names like London Bridge, Sevenoaks and Tonbridge don't quite have the ring of the Mystic East.

Our train was also a bit longer than that strangely truncated version shown in the film, and those extra coaches were useful when one of racing's shiftier characters just happened to jump into the carriage as we pulled out of Waterloo. Not that he could compare with the sort of guys they used to make public "do-not-play-cards-with-strangers" announcements about on the Brighton train. The last fleecing I remember was of a group of jockeys who lured a mug-like-looking stranger into a game of poker. They didn't realise they were sheep that had invited the wolf into the fold until they handed him the pack to deal. He slowly stretched the whole deck like a conjuror, and it was a wiser but poorer group that stumbled over the station bridge an hour later.

A race train is always an amazing mixture of different elements kaleidoscoped together for one day's mission. In one carriage on Thursday there is an actress, a spiv, three jockeys, a journalist and an art dealer. Not as good as eight maids a milking, perhaps, but not bad. Actress Susan Jameson has come to see her horse, Indian Cottage, deliver the goods in the Aldington Handicap Chase. "It's a wonderful antidote to acting," she says. "Marvellous outdoor optimism."

Looking less optimistic is Graham Thorner, champion jockey three years ago, and second in the list at the moment. But he explains that his mood comes only from the thought of having to "do" 9st 13lb the next day. Yet he warms to the company as he tells of his own personal disaster on the road to Nottingham on Monday: "I wound down the window to clear my throat—and spat my teeth out!"

Discussions turn inevitably to the possibilities of the coming afternoon. "Just need a couple of monkeys to get me arter trubble," mutters one unlucky punter.

Overleaf: Unspeakable in pursuit of the uneatable. The top hat may be absurd (and is certainly no protection) but in January 1981 John Thorne was the story and the hunting field was the only place to get it (Chris Smith)

We hope his heart stands up to the strain, because when we have got off the train and meet the course doctor, he tells us of the racegoer recently brought to the ambulance room: "I tried to listen to his heart but, wherever I put the stethoscope, all I could hear was galloping hooves."

More learned discussion before the first race. Can't back the favourite, we decide, "too dodgy". Favourite canters up despite trying to turn left after the last jump into the paddock goldfish pond. Winner is long-toothed eight-year-old, and study of racecard reveals his sire as the horse on which I won my first race twelve years ago. I notice policemen are looking younger.

See even more crumpled-looking figure of "The Dodger," long-time "punter of the year" in National Hunt racing. "He's doing himself to death, old Dodge," mutters an ageing little side-kick as the deep-coated, smoke-glassed figure opines on the next race. "He keeps burning it both ends . . . it will never last."

Dodger denies it. "I only goes to bed with the *Sporting Life* these days," he says and agrees that we can't back the favourite in the next. "Only ran two days ago, and it will never give the weight to China Bank."

Favourite wins in canter. All other Press men and loyal supporters of trainer Auriol Sinclair do some mutual congratulations. Our own conclave of Turf geniuses now decide that the Gifford-trained favourite is a good thing in the next, ignoring advice of little old "Nately" Yardley that King Flame "only has to jump round." He does. So decide not to risk money on Gifford runner, Flying Orchid, in the "boys' race". Flying Orchid wins so far that he nearly laps the others.

Disgust softened by champagne, generosity of owner Mr Luck. Hope this has healing qualities for son of owner, whose luck has so run out that his face looks like an advert for seat belts.

At last the time for big punt on actress's horse, Indian Cottage. Acrobat jockey Andy Turnell has arrived after train delays. Learned study of Indian Cottage's backside assures us that he is "in great nick". In the race, outsider Parkgate Inn makes attempt on world speed record. Indian Cottage finds fences coming up too fast, and finally hurls Turnell to the ground. Miss Jameson plays Victorian lady with style. Doctor's twelve-year-old daughter utters four-letter curse. Doctor looks down anxiously: "How much did you have on?"

One more race before the 3.34 from Westerhanger. Ace pundits all agree that Inventory is the biggest certainty since Income Tax. Get delayed on way to bookmaker; fail to get on. So, of course, Inventory wins in canter.

Fifteen minutes later jockeys, Miss Jameson, journalists and the dope-test assistant are all crammed into one carriage. By Ashford, Turnell has taken his second pound off her. "Turning the knife in the wound," she demurs sweetly. She is not the only loser. So I go on down to the saltier part of the train.

We are passing through the Weald of Kent. Green fields, twilight and oast-houses. A long way from crises, but one little old friend is bemoaning his bad luck: "Yer can't make a living at this nah. It's all the exes. I have been doing it for 24 years, and I think I shall have to give up and get a job. Nobody cares about twenty or thirty professional punters." Then, with magnificent scorn: "Racing belongs to the multitude nah."

We arrived at Waterloo, and "the multitude" were queueing for the trains home. Full of woes, maybe some of them in need of escape. You can't run, but on a race train you can certainly hide.

There's another place you can hide. It tends to be a bit colder and in some senses more risky, but in another more peaceful and serene. It's out on the back of a race horse in the morning. In my earlier jockey's life there had always been a delicious sense of escape as the string trotted off towards the gallops just as the commuters rushed for the train. But of all those mornings, none paid off as well as this one, two seasons after I swopped the whip for the pen. In its own little way it was as near a "scoop" as we ever had. Anyway, it's one to tell the grandchildren—even if they have to look in my old Victorian mother's scrap book. Her no-nonsense version has the first sentences omitted.

The ultimate in sitting on a story. Brough Scott aboard Red Rum on a rainy morning in November 1975 (Gerry Cranham)

Brief Encounter with a Star
November 1975

It was like suddenly finding yourself in bed with a film star. Would she be as fantastic as you imagined? And would you match up to her the way you had in your dreams? The salty rain-swept emptiness of Southport sands at 8.15 last Wednesday morning was a pretty odd place for an assignation with a star, but in racing terms the rest of the comparison was accurate. For I was riding Red Rum.

Red Rum? Yes, *the* Red Rum, winner of the 1973 and 1974 Grand Nationals, all in all the most charismatic National Hunt horse since Arkle. Yet here he was cantering beneath me, and about a hundred miles of sand ahead for us.

The first feel of Red Rum is a little disappointing. He seems a shade narrow and lightweight, much more ex-flat racehorse than big strong 'chaser. But then "ex-flat racehorse" is exactly what he is, having started out eight seasons ago with a dead heat at that same Liverpool track he has since taken by storm.

It was old pro's weather on Wednesday morning. Solid Lancashire rain only eased to a threatening drizzle as we left the little yard at the back of McCain's Car Sales, out on to the Aughton Road and through the streets of the Birkdale part of Southport until we finally came to the beach with its warning notice: "Drivers beware of soft sand."

You can't imagine a style of exercising racehorses further removed from the traditional Indian-file-up-the-lane-to-the-downs style. Horses walking in a cluster, Red Rum in front, with his lad Billy Ellison beside us on the big, white-faced Glenkiln, past the pet centre and the Chinese fish and chip shop, over the level-crossing and the main road. It certainly works for Red Rum. And in trying to explain it, I remembered another time when, hoisted on well-lubricated words from the night before, I accompanied another champion in training. That was with Chris Finnegan, running round the early morning streets of Clerkenwell. When I eventually gasped back to his door, he told me that he enjoyed the bustle and greeting of the town, and I don't think it all fanciful to say that this equine hero feels the same. So we were safely on to the beach, and after the briefest of instructions were cantering in pairs southwards along "the gallop", a newly harrowed stretch of sand between seaweed and waves.

At first, the impression of "ex-flat horse" remained. "I'm not sure that I would feel that confident going to Becher's on this," was the way I put it to myself. But then, as the sands swept by, there came a feeling of relentless power about the stride. We seemed to have been cantering for about five miles, and although I hadn't ridden for a few months, I thought I was showing plenty of the old magic. ("What magic?" asked an unkind friend with an all too clear memory of my brief career in the saddle.) "Do we pull up now?" I called across to Billy Ellison. "Oh no," came the reply. "We've got a *long* way to go yet."

Suddenly there was a threat of disaster. Alone with a film star, I was going to ruin everything by being sick. Then of all things, on this beach a hundred miles from nowhere, there was a hoot on a car horn, and right beside us was Ginger McCain. "He means us to go a bit quicker," shouted Billy.

This wasn't going to be funny, for you know that as you release the brake a little the load becomes greater. Far from a beaten-up ex-flat horse, the length and power of Red Rum's stride made me feel that he might win next year's National pulling a cart, let alone an unfit and panicky journalist. One more notch and we would have gone. But then an angel in the unlikely form of Billy Ellison saved us. "Whoa up! that's it," he called. Red Rum eased up knowing where he was all the time, and in a couple of minutes we were across the sand and into the sea.

Yes, into the sea! All McCain's horses go into the sea, and Red Rum, who had previously suffered from the usually incurable foot disease of pedalostitis, owes much of his dramatic improvement to his regular exercise in sea and on sand. "He hates trotting on the road, you know," said Billy. "When he works he likes to get another horse ahead of him so that he can sort of get it in his sights and then come and do it at the finish. Watch him going home. He always likes to buck opposite the convent." He did, and plenty more, and having spent one and a half fantasy-come-true hours on Red Rum's back, it is my pleasure and privilege to report that his spirit is burning strong.

At least there wasn't much dishonour in that Red Rum memory. But in the midwinter of '78 the mind was going back to other times when some of the behaviour would be best forgotten. In this case we were lucky to have anything left to forget.

Two Beauties and the Beast on the Hill
February 12th 1978

The big freeze has shivered all horse racing to a halt, and every eager racing man is kicking himself for not having fixed up a trip to Cagnes-sur-Mer, in the South of France. That's where we went ten years ago, and a couple of different moves one starry Riviera night could have changed one of jump racing's most famous records, and might even have led me to an examination of France's esteemed prison system—from the inside.

Now I have got nothing against the Hippodrome de la Côte d'Azur. With the blue of the Mediterranean in front of you and the snow-capped peaks of the Alpes Maritimes up behind, it is one of the most beautiful, as well as most efficient, racecourses in the world. It is just that even the Entente Cordiale can be messed up if you fail to hold your liquor or learn the lingo. On that occasion our team, who were down there because of the foot-and-mouth outbreak in England, had not been unsuccessful. David Nicholson had won the Prix de Bouif on Cavalry Charge and, at six foot in his tights, had been dubbed Le Plus Grand

Jockey du Monde, and Irish champion Bobby Coonan had been the first to secure a close personal relationship with a young French lady. So that Saturday evening Stan Mellor and I were aiming to help things along, he because of his natural charm and I to avoid the attentions of one disgruntled and extremely dusky French punter who had lost money on me that afternoon.

We seemed to have made a particular friend of a snappily dressed little jockey who never rode very much but was a dab hand with the champagne bottle. Our friend appeared to be insisting that we accompany him and another jockey to a special dinner that night. The restaurant was set high up in the hills, with all the lights of Nice bobbing below, and it was only after we had been taken to the place of honour among some three hundred guests that we noticed something odd about the lay-out. The whole place was built around and above a little sandy square which looked exactly like the stock Mexican setting for a TV western.

Our hosts continued to lavish such hospitality on us that we suspected no problems and when, after the fifteenth course and 25th glass we were asked to go down to the square for *les photographes*, we dismissed the knowing smiles of our fellow guests as a salute to dear old Britannia. But suddenly our friend had disappeared, the door of the courtyard opened and there stood a mighty behorned beast breathing fire and brimstone and apparently holding us personally responsible for all the wrongs done to the bovine species down the ages.

They said afterwards it was only a heifer, but when the beast all but changed Stan Mellor's epitaph from The First Man to Ride a Thousand Winners to The First Jockey to Die in the Bullring, and then hit the wooden post next to me with a splintering crash, it was time to take evasive action. With his champion jockey's

Riviera revels. Brough Scott and a 'weary' Stan Mellor whoop it up above Nice, January 1968, but it nearly ended in tears

reactions, Stan found the way first and on my desk today I still have a photo of the intrepid Mellor shinned up a tree with a thin-faced B. Scott grinning drunkenly beside him. There is also another photo of us, riding a donkey, and here's the twist. Our two friends are also in the picture, and are all too clearly identifiable as two of the gang who a few years later served prison sentences for their part in France's most notorious "fixed" race, the Prix Bride Abattue, and our champagne-opener was proved to be a hit man for the Mafia.

Those were risks we didn't have to take. Now to dangers that every jump jockey has to face—and often unnecessarily. It's a situation that rankled when I was riding, when the piece was written, and it still rankles today.

Novice Chase Disgrace
November 20th 1977

Steeplechasing is a risky business. And novice 'chases are the riskiest of all. Yet every week brings instances of men and horses being sent out to take these risks with little or no preparation. In what has become a million-viewer national sport, these cases are an intolerable disgrace.

Our pictures show what can happen even to fully prepared horses and jockeys, all of whom mercifully survived more or less intact. The grey horse, Frederick John, already had five novice 'chase placings to his credit and 29-year-old John Williams had the experience of riding more than a hundred jumping winners. "We had a beautiful clear run to the fence," says Williams, "but he slipped on take-off, slid into the bottom and just somersaulted over it." Behind him the 33-year-old David Cartwright (two hundred winners), on the untried but Tim

The risks they take. John Williams (from No.8) and David Cartwright (No.11) crash at Worcester in November 1977. Novice Chases can be dangerous things (Chris Smith)

Forster-schooled Island Prince, jumped the fence perfectly but "just had no-where to land."

Neither Williams, who resumed yesterday after being—understatement of the year—"a bit crushed and bruised", nor Cartwright is in any way cowed by the prospect of more novice 'chase rides, but they share the general disgust that so many horses and jockeys go round in them unprepared. "I don't mind novice 'chases," says Williams in his stuttering Welsh scrum-half way. "In fact, I prefer them to some scatty three-year-olds you get in hurdles. But there have been dozens of occasions when I have ridden a horse that hasn't been schooled at all. I ride a lot in Scandinavia in the summer, and there you can't run a horse in a novice 'chase without first schooling on a racecourse in front of a steward. I think we should have some system like that here."

Cartwright was more doubtful about changing regulations merely to include horses, pointing out that very often it's the riders that are the hazard. "If there are plenty of runners, you hope to find someone sensible to track," he says. "But then your heart sinks when you see it's some kamikaze pilot up in front of you."

One of my own most vivid riding experiences concerned being down at the start of a novice 'chase at Devon and Exeter some eight years ago, and seeing a lad who only six months before I had known as a kid who couldn't ride a gallop, let alone a "school". He was on a wild-looking black beast, and had the ashen, haunted look of a boy soldier in the trenches. I did what I could in the way of "grab hold of its head and look after yourself" encouragement, but it wasn't much use. He got over only three fences before it buried him.

Maybe I should have reported the trainer concerned, but at least nowadays official steps are being taken to make trainers responsible for the rides they give their lads, and the jockeys have, in Ron Atkins, a spokesman who is prepared to keep hammering away at abuses such as persistent fallers.

"The Trainers' Association and the Jockeys' Association are in total agree-ment in the need for a National Hunt apprentice scheme," said Atkins. "And when it comes in, it should go a long way towards stopping the carrot of a few bad-race rides being used as a bait to keep lads quiet. I think the standard of riding, apart from the top twenty jockeys and the twenty or so up-and-coming lads, is terrible these days, and it's only going to improve if trainers give young jockeys decent rides rather than putting them up on what can be a lethal weapon to them and to others in the race."

Of course, there are plenty of cases of the unschooled horse and greenhorn jockey jumping round successfully. But at Leicester recently an animal fell a few minutes after his young rider had confessed to a top jockey that his horse had never even seen a fence. If I were that horse's owner, I would at once take the animal from its present trainer and send him to one of the many others who spend painstaking hours schooling their charges. If I were the stewards, I would ban seven-pound claimers from novice 'chases, and keep a rigid check on persistent fallers. But there's something else, stronger and far less bureaucratic, which if properly active should make all this unnecessary. It's called conscience.

Nothing much has happened since that was written to make me think that the situation has improved a great deal. But of course there are times when the lack of navigation ability comes through circumstances, or through a jockey's carelessness. This is a time, not the first, nor I fear the last, when the mouth was some way ahead of the man.

Sharpen up your Somersaulting Technique
March 29th 1981

Be warned, even Grand National words can endanger your health. Just mention those Aintree fences when I was riding, and down we went four times out of four, and on one occasion not even in a race.

Of course, those were the days when men were men and fences were fences, a statement that can now be made in the saloon-bar certainty that this time around the BBC won't try and help me prove it. For while next Saturday Julian Wilson will be the hawk-eyed linch-pin behind the Beeb's five-hour, twenty-camera, two hundred-man Grand National coverage, back in 1970 he was just a young thruster with the brilliant idea that the Aintree fences could be better understood if a couple of jockeys with microphones attached rode over them the Thursday prior to the big day. Since this had never been done before, Wilson's first problem was volunteers. For reasons which may have escaped him, but which had a lot to do with a hundred pounds, I became the first mug, and after several household names had declined the offer, the great Pat McCarron agreed as well.

Pat had two big things going for him: a superb Grand National record (second on Freddie in both 1964 and 1965), and a reliable horse (Limetra, who had been round Aintree many times). In the event, I had neither, because two jumpers had dropped out lame (one of them Polaris Missile, mother of Spartan Missile), and so we had to rely on the Great Wilson Replacement Scheme. One look in the paddock and you feared the worst. Limetra was having the batteries and wires fitted to his saddle-cloth with the long-suffering calm of a horse who had already run that afternoon, but my beast, Babur Bay, was dragging his lad round the ring with such eye-bulging ferocity that a puff of smoke from his nostrils and he could have auditioned for the Brothers Grimm. Being in the saddle only confirmed the problem and, worse still, with the BBC men checking their watches as only a TV crew can, there was a suggestion that we should start at once.

It's a long trek from the Grand National start to the first fence, and I can tell you it's no route to take on a horse with steam coming out of its ears. So, despite the tea-break grumbles, we got dispensation to go back and jump the relatively easy final two fences to warm up or, in my horse's case, to cool down. This showed two things—that Limetra was safe but shattered, and that while you could hold Babur Bay going towards a fence, five strides away and you had lift-off.

The idea was for us to chat our way round a complete circuit while the cameras lingered on every move. In my years as a jockey there were other moments of pressure, but none bigger than this: all the BBC's cameras and tracker trucks poised, the genuine Grand National obstacles cold-bloodedly up ahead, and me sitting on a lunatic intent on trying for the world long-jump record at every fence.

It didn't last that long. We were all right going to the first, Pat McCarron chatting away and Babur Bay reasonably anchored, but at the obstacle Limetra popped middle-agedly over while Babur Bay threw himself half way to Haydock, and only a series of jawbreakers pulled him back to Limetra before we launched off at the second. As most of the seven hundred million TV audience know, those first two fences may have a drop on the landing side but they are a sloping, inviting inch on take-off. The third fence is different, a solid two-foot guard-rail in front, a gaping ditch and then this great gorse cliff towering beyond it. The best idea seemed to be to forget Limetra, and ask Babur Bay to help himself. It didn't work. If he did three somersaults, I did seven, and lay on Aintree's hallowed turf cursing the BBC and all her works.

As it happened, we were eventually re-united and, no small thanks to Pat McCarron and Limetra, completed a full Grand National circuit. But not before I was asked one of the questions of a lifetime. With all his glittering TV prospects crashing with me, Julian Wilson sped like a long dog after Babur Bay, caught him at the Canal Turn and finally brought him to where B. Scott was spitting his way back to consciousness. Then, with the whites of his eyes just betraying how much it meant to him, "Wislon" looked at the mud-bespattered quadruped, glanced back to where Becher's, Valentine's and the others beckoned, and uttered the immortal line: "Do you think it will have taught him a lesson?"

As a matter of fact the postscript to the story is that Babur Bay had indeed learnt a little and he then went round like a pussycat. The only snag came after we had jumped the Chair Fence, got rather over-bold taking the water jump to complete the circuit . . . and suddenly had a hideous moment as we headed off towards the Melling Road again, and the brakes didn't seem to be working at all.

That whole episode was an example of the rashness of making brave declarations late at night. But after-hours revelry has not always slowed jockeys down . . . witness this week in October 1980.

Late Night Training
October 26th 1980

All those who feel that sportsmen should be tucked up in bed before the ten o'clock news were struck a bitter blow last week by the performances of Soaf, Pelayo and Allibar. No, not the Tunisian badminton team, but the three horses who earned racing immortality by carting Willie Shoemaker and Prince Charles around to enormous public acclaim. But well-merited though this was, with Shoemaker winning on Soaf and Pelayo at Sandown and Prince Charles finishing a gallant second on Allibar at Ludlow, I have to reveal that neither hero obeyed the ten o'clock curfew beloved by training manuals.

Without a mole in the palace garden, it's impossible fully to check the Prince's evening. But Friday's 31-line Court Circular showed that his helicoptered multi-engagement Thursday had ended with a film première which presumably meant lights out not much before midnight. As the last time I had a movie night in London before riding at Ludlow ended with my falling off in a two-horse race, the Prince's wholly admirable second place is just one more galling proof of his infinite parachuting, submarining, sound-barrier-breaking superiority.

But enough of Charles's eve-of-match activities. What about the tiny American, Willie Shoemaker, who to my certain knowledge was indulging in rich food and alcoholic liquor until nigh midnight at Tuesday's Chivas Regal banquet? And then, while we hacks were stumbling home, he and his lovely lofty wife, Cindy, were hoofing around the floor of Tramp before he was shunted down to Sandown Park at eight o'clock in the morning to try out the racetrack.

Admittedly, at 6st 12lb in colours, 49-year-old Willie the Shoe doesn't have any weight worries, but the old adage about alcohol and insomnia taking the edge off physical performance took a knock from the Americans' resounding victory in the team event against Great Britain, and from Shoemaker's two tremendous untipped personal successes.

To be honest, some jockeys have been disproving this rule for years. Of course, they need to be very fit men in the first place, and have to be a lot more abstemious than Bill Scott (no relation), who lost the 1846 Derby when all too obviously "drunk in charge". But in a sport where the horse does the actual running, and where the morale of the jockey is all-important, the occasional eve-of-ride night out isn't necessarily harmful. The problems only begin to crowd in when night is extended to morning.

The most famous recent case was after Ron Barry won the Cheltenham Gold Cup on The Dikler in 1973. By the time he approached the first flight of hurdles at Uttoxeter next afternoon, assorted "hairs of the dog" put so many images in his retina that the great man deemed it wise to jump each flight with his eyes closed. The victory which followed must remain one of the most remarkable in "big Ron's" still-active career, which is now approaching the 750-winner mark.

The pair who almost lost a walk-over. Brough Scott and Patrol canter to the start (Provincial Press Agency)

So, too, must be the problem diagnosed by the doctor who was called hurriedly to the sick bay after that Uttoxeter triumph. "What's wrong, Barry? Is it serious?" asked the medic. "Oh, no," said the hungover champion, "it's the drink taken. My head's killing me. Do you have any Alka Seltzer?"

My only experience of riding seriously under the influence was also successful, but a deal less heroic since it was a walk-over. That was at Kempton, so there was the glorious chance of lunching in London first and then taking the high road to the races with the heady thought of a certain winner.

The first part of the plan worked all too well, so pulling on boots and breeches became a major test of mind and muscle. But eventually one well-wined jockey tottered into the paddock to complete the formalities, which even in a steeplechase consist merely of cantering over the finish line. Unfortunately, no one had told the horse, who kept rushing round the paddock with every symptom of an imminent nervous breakdown. Riding him out past the stands suddenly became something even a sober jockey would not have fancied.

Luckily I succeeded, or there would be no escaping the epitaph: The Jockey Who Lost A Walkover.

That may have been all good gossip column fun but you can't wander around the racing parish for long without feeling the gulf between those top table antics and the less privileged members of the workforce in the lads' canteen. The first, easy, gut reaction is to look at the Rolls Royces in the owners' car park and the conditions in some lads' hostels and demand the return of the guillotine. But it's not quite as simple as that. The exact figures in the piece below may have changed but I doubt if the principles have. It's a problem for us all.

Racing's Catch 22—a Dickensian Nightmare
November 30th 1980

Only one trainer in recent years has tackled his profession's biggest problem head-on. He sacked his stablelads and exercised his horses by chasing them around a field in a car. Fortunately for industrial relations, none of them won and our man went broke.

Today, with soaring food and fuel costs, and the lads' paltry £30 wage of four years ago doubled, there are many of Britain's 1,000 hard-working racehorse trainers who secretly crave for a similarly drastic, if more successful, system. And in a disturbing number of cases that craving has come all too close to fact.

Only on Friday, a twenty-year-old Lancashire lad told me how he joined a Midland stable last spring to find that he, another apprentice and a sixteen-year-old non-riding school leaver were the only staff to look after eighteen horses. All three slept in the same room, two in the same bed, and throughout his four months' stay, his gross wages were kept at least £20 below the national agreed minimum from 1 August, £63 a week.

"To be honest, it were a right shambles. It were against all that I have been taught," said the lad, who had previously done two spells at the apprentice training school, four years at a leading Berkshire yard and is now at home receiving £24 a fortnight on the dole. "The horses were only out fifteen minutes, and they did rear and bite more than in other stables, but I went along with everything because I were getting the race-rides."

He has asked for his name not to be used because, surprisingly but revealingly, he wants to get back into racing and fears being branded as a troublemaker. He is, of course, just one isolated case, but there are likely to be many others. "Last year we sent a confidential questionnaire to the 200 conditional NH jockeys among our members," said Geoffrey Summers, secretary of the Jockeys' Association, "and the replies indicated that 27 per cent of them were getting less than the agreed minimum wage of £53."

Let it be quite clearly stated that nobody in authority approves of it. The Trainers' Association, the Jockey Club, the Stablelads' Association and the Transport and General Workers' Union will all open their palms in sincerity, and point to the agreement negotiated by the National Joint Council for Stable Wages, and so anyone not getting the agreed minimum wage should just let them know. "We have now had four years of agreements," said Tommy Delaney of the SLA, "and the excuse of ignorance by either party really should not be good enough." To which Sam Horncastle of the Cambridgeshire TGWU adds: "Everyone is getting the full wage at Newmarket. If there are any lads griping in pubs or clubs around the country, they're doing it in the wrong place. They should come to Tommy or me completely confidential, and we can go through the agreed procedure to get things sorted out."

So that's it then. All we have to do is to make sure all underpaid lads take one step forward, rogue trainers pay up, Dickensian shame is lifted and we can all go and have a jar. Well, it's not quite as easy as that. For a start, very, very few trainers are rogues, and most of them, the one in the Lancashire lad's case included, work long hours in poor conditions for the sort of money that turns sedentary journalists back to the bar in embarrassment.

If you look at the figures computed by Peter Jones of Trainers' Record, it is brutally clear that not many trainers are making anything except ulcers. Of the 370 licensed on the Flat last season, only 83 had more than ten winners, and of only 420 trainers and 600 permit holders on the far more financially pressed jumping scene, only 58 passed the ten-winner total. In many cases it is all too obvious that much more strain will send them under, and in the most difficult Catch-22 of any receding labour market, some employees can feel that if they take more money they may destroy their own jobs.

Any willingness on that score is compounded by the best and worst feature that underpins the whole racing set-up in Britain—that 95 per cent of working stable labour comes into the game dreaming of being a jockey. It's best because it means that there is—at the start at any rate—an obsessive dedication to the job, and because the emphasis on riding makes the average English lad ride far better than his counterpart anywhere in the world. It's worst because the vast majority who don't make jockeys are very often left with a touch of resentment, which contributes to the catastrophic drop-out rate in the early twenties, and the sadly high proportion of floating labour drifting from one stable to another.

But if the good trainer can sometimes have a legitimate grouse about the standard of his lads, the whole glorious profession will surely ruin its name if it fails to pay lads agreed wages, or abuses the well-intentioned conditional NH jockey scheme whereby, as on the Flat, a trainer gets half the £32 riding fee every time his young protégé has a mount.

The only excuses can be those two well-established fellow travellers, ignorance and unreality. Ignorance should be put overboard at once, but when you think what a huge persuasive member of the crew unreality has become, you have to wonder whether we will ever make it walk the plank. Can we afford not to?

Anguish as we may (and must) about the inner social grace of the racing game, the sad fact is that it's the outward physical sign which is usually noticed. For those of us who work on TV, this outer sign sometimes seems to be everything. Anyway here's the view of June 1982.

Taking the Mike
June 1982

If Benjamin Disraeli were alive today, he would surely be the TV star of the political stage, able to escape from the trickiest impasse with his famous dictum: "Never complain, and never explain." Wise words, no doubt, but then Dizzy didn't have to wrestle with hours of "live" sports coverage, action replays and the ever-present danger of making a "Colemanballs".

For those of us who jump through the commentating hoops, it will be a long hot summer trying to avoid Private Eye's list of *mots injustes* founded by such gems as the line the eponymous David used about the great Cuban runner in the 1976 Olympics: "Now Juantorena opens his legs and shows his class." Justice is not always done, for after several seasons of stirring banalities I made the list only with an admittedly typical but actually falsely attributed statement: "Here comes the unmistakable shape of Lester Piggott—er—or is it Joe Mercer?"

Yet the irretrievability of the mischosen phrase really comes second in TV hazards to the waking nightmare of finding yourself physically, as well as verbally, stranded on the beach. One interview with that restlessly pacing trainer, Peter Walwyn, came to a yelping halt when I strayed too far from the anchoring sound box to which my ear-piece was attached. And on another occasion, an otherwise fascinating talk with some racing dignitary was completely lost to the listening world because the microphone turned out to be a rolled-up copy of the *Sporting Life*.

Of course, the huge popularity of the *It'll be all right on the Night* series is because the unsolicited absurdity is always waiting in the wings, as we discovered at Newmarket one day when the French champion, Yves St Martin, came on and jabbered away nineteen words to the dozen, unfortunately not one of them in English. Yet a very real part of the amusement is the come-uppance for moments that appear to be taking themselves too seriously.

This is particularly true with sport, where the emphasis over the years has been to look very much on the sunniest side of the street: "And it is an especially warm welcome to another fascinating game (race, match, set, frame or whatever)." That is an attitude much-criticised, but while it must be right to clear out the more ludicrous type, critics sometimes don't realise how different the role of reporter and commentator can be.

For while nobody wants to read bland, boring, syrupy reports or prodigally strewn superlatives, it is not easy to hold your TV audience by coming on the screen and telling the absolute negative truth about how dull and boring an afternoon might be in store. It is also quite difficult to hang on to your job. After I announced that the runners for the "seller" at Catterick some years ago were vying for the title of the worst horse in Britain, it seemed for a while as if it was going to be back to humping muck sacks to eke out the extra crusts.

It is a personal view that sports commentators have grown up considerably in recent times, which is hardly surprising, since they are still mewling and puking infants compared with the written reports which must have been going since some Hellenic front page was first "held" for the Olympic Games three-and-a-half thousand years ago.

None the less, commentaries are still beset by pressures to enthuse rather than analyse. If sports writers had to hand over to a commercial break in the middle of an article, would they all avoid promising every excitement bar the Apocalypse "in just a couple of minutes"? And would they really be so dull at heart that they wouldn't become excited at the possibilities, rather than the actualities, of the event they had in front of them?

But then, perhaps, they are too wary of the horrors that can befall those who seek to invest the fleeting moment with an importance it may not warrant. One freezing cold afternoon at Harringay greyhounds I was doing a replay of what had been a supremely uneventful dog race, with the favourite leading from the second favourite throughout. In an orgy of passion, I compared the winner with every canine from Glasgow Billy to Rin Tin Tin, only to discover, five exhausted seconds after hailing him over the finishing line , that it was a marathon race, and there was a whole circuit still to run.

Disraeli might not have appreciated the moment, but anyone who does sports commentaries just has to console himself with the words of a present-day peer, Lord Longford: "There are worse things in life than being a figure of fun."

Those were reflections on events in the public gaze. They have their moments, but over the past ten years no on-screen problem matched the unexpected drama of one July morning in 1983. It had set out to be a pleasant, if routine, trip to see the filly Time Charter work in preparation for what was to be a winning run in the next Saturday's King George VI and Queen Elizabeth II Stakes at Ascot. Jockey Billy Newnes was later to get a couple of years' suspension for accepting a £1000 gift from a notorious punter. That was Billy's silly mistake. What follows is the other sort of risk. It's not your fault, and it gives no warnings.

Billy Newnes over the Styx
July 17th 1983

Billy Newnes turned easily in the saddle and looked across the gallops towards White Horse Hill. The rest of the string would be out of the way in a second or two, and he and Malcolm could work their two animals up the long, green stretch of Berkshire turf. Nothing to it. Nothing except that within a minute it would look as if Billy's next ride would be across the River Styx.

At that moment last Thursday morning Billy Newnes had as much right to think that the world was smiling on him as any 23-year-old in the whole of heatwave-hit Britain. Now first jockey to Henry Candy's successful stable high on the ancient Ridgeway at Kingstone Warren, ten miles west of Wantage, Newnes, in black riding boots and red velvet crash hat, looked very much the rising star who had shot to fame last year by winning the Oaks and the Champion Stakes on Time Charter.

The two horses set off, to the casual observer a perfect example of the rippling athletic strength of the thoroughbred in action, but to the little man on the grey it was but a three-cylinder imitation of the real power he wanted to use next Saturday when Time Charter runs in Ascot's £120,000 King George VI and Queen Elizabeth Diamond Stakes, the most important all-aged race of the year. Billy wanted to make up for the uncharacteristically slow-witted ride he had given Time Charter when only sixth in the Eclipse Stakes last time, and was sure that the white-nosed lady with the short, purposeful, clockwork stride was right back to her best.

But all that was ahead. The job in hand was to make Silver Venture stretch as he came past the Stone Age burial mound used as a vantage point by Henry Candy and your correspondent. When they had passed us, the jockeys began to pull up, the trainer to turn away to other duties. Then disaster struck; a dreadful sequence still frozen in the retina. Silver Venture staggered, somersaulted at three-quarter gallop and suddenly there were two stricken creatures, and I was running across the grass.

When I reached them, Silver Venture was already dead, a terrible haemor-rhage gushing from his nose, and Billy Newnes was making a ghastly noise through his teeth, blood leaking from his mouth and ear. By the time I'd got the helmet off, Henry Candy had driven up in the Landrover, taken one look, said calmly, "This is an ambulance job," and sped off to telephone.

Then things got even worse. Billy stopped writhing, and went completely limp. I'd never given the kiss of life before—indeed, the only person I've seen die was my father—but here on this perfect July morning, with only the larksong for company, it was all too clear that W. Newnes was on his way to becoming an ex-jockey. His watch showed ten minutes past eight.

It may have been only a minute. It seemed like an eternity. No feeling, no pulse, the eyes rolled up into the head. Then one long, dreadful breath, and limp again. Desperately, I pushed and blew. Another breath came, and slowly, like some stubborn pump, another and another until at last they began to settle to a rhythm.

The rest is simply told. Billy came round at 8.20 and almost wished he hadn't. Later inspection was to reveal a broken collar-bone and damaged ribs, but nothing bad enough to prevent his going home on Friday. The Wantage ambulance did brilliantly to arrive at 8.33. Henry Candy, the very symbol of coolness under pressure, saw his jockey rushed to hospital and began the task of ringing Billy's wife, Silver Venture's owner and the knacker's yard to get the dead horse off the hill.

W. Newnes won't ride for a few weeks. He will have to sit at home and rest the collar-bone and his aching ribs. He'll hate that. But it's an awful lot better than Hades.

7.The Horse at the heart of it all

However much we may cloak the fact with other details, the abiding mystery about horse-racing is that it is a form of athletics where the athletes can't talk. Here are just a few of the dumb friends who puzzled and pleased us over the years. Looking back at them makes me realize how much we owe them all. It would be nice to tell them some time, even if, as in this first case, you had to speak in French.

Dahlia—A Chantilly Bloom
August 18th 1974

What special ingredients of flesh, blood and temperament make up a champion? If we could analyse one, surely we could foresee another and then it might be Goodbye, mortgage. Hello, Hawaii.

If you are interested, your last certain chance to see the real McCoy will come on Tuesday when Dahlia will pop across the Channel to run in the Benson and Hedges Gold Cup at York. She is a champion by any standards. She has won in France, Ireland, England and the USA and her latest win at Ascot took her past Mill Reef's all-time European stakes winnings of £300,000.

Yet she may have plenty more to come from what Maurice Zilber said to me last week in France. "After York (worth a mere £50,000) she will go for the Arc and may well race next year as a five-year-old. That would be very interesting."

But what makes her different? It can't be that she is perfectly bred by Arc winner, Vaguely Noble out of an ultra tough American mare that ran 71 times. It isn't that she is the best looking horse that you will ever see on a racecourse. So there must be something about her that those closest to her at Chantilly could explain. The first impression in the early morning sun of last Wednesday was that if they had a phenomenon on their hands they were being pretty casual about it. Maurice Zilber was away supervising runners at Deauville and his so dependable 62-year-old assistant Henri Nicholas didn't exactly rush over when Dahlia was brought out of her box by her sad-eyed Egyptian lad Cesar Hami. Nor did he fret when the original moustachioed French onion seller called Jacques Houssa swung on to her back and rode long-legged, casual-cowboy style across the yard. Nor would you be that struck by Dahlia's appearance. She is not particularly strong in front, her neck is not high set and muscular.

But three things you would have to admit. First that her coat gleams like no polish can give. Second that as she walks away from you her hindquarters give a tremendous impression of power; and third, and what you remember most, is the quizzical intelligence of the concave Araby head.

The statistics speak of that power, yet what does it feel like? In the yard on Wednesday was Henri Mathelin, for years one of the very best French jump jockeys but also light enough to ride on the flat.

Overleaf: All action at Newbury (Chris Smith)

"She has no great stretch in her stride in front of her," he said, "but when you

Lester Piggott and Dahlia are led in by the mare's Egyptian lad, Cesar Hami, after their triumph in the King George VI and Queen Elizabeth Stakes, July 1974 (Sport and General)

ask her to go, you feel the muscles really work at the back and she is like a bullet. I saw her last race at Ascot and as Piggott eased her out she accelerated so fast that for a few strides she took him by surprise. I am sure of it."

But earlier this season she either hasn't wanted or hasn't been able to go. She was unplaced on her first two outings and only third in the Coronation Cup. The dogs were barking for Zilber and many still find it hard to give credit.

After she had moved down the field at Ascot I came here with one of our most experienced experts. "I can't understand that man," he said. "He runs her when she is not right, if anyone else did that it would finish a horse, with him it puts them right."

Zilber, needless to say, just spreads his hands with pleasure. "The big prizes are at this end of the summer," he says. "She is a filly and she was not coming to herself until this time. But you have looked at her now. She is well, isn't she? She is very brilliant, very intelligent but she is a lady of caprice." he says. "It is the aura of a great star, sometimes she won't go on to the gallops and we just have to wait, maybe ten minutes. She needs to be understood." So her greatest quality is also the least tangible. But it is the same that usually separates human champions from the rest. It is the nervous force and will to win. Unfortunately, for that trip to Hawaii, you can only recognise it *after* they have won.

*Dahlia duly pottered across to York and picked up the
Benson and Hedges a week after that piece was written and
retired at the end of the next season with a then record
winnings total. In 1984 her son Dahar was a top-class colt
in France, taking the prestigious Prix Lupin in May and the
French Derby in June.
Our next hero was a gelding so could leave no such legacy.
But he certainly didn't lack character.*

Captain Christy and Mr Hyde
November 30th 1975

Dr Jekyll wasn't showing a trace of Mr Hyde down in County Kildare on Wednesday. In fact, to watch him with little Elaine Taaffe on his back you would think Captain Christy more the seaside donkey than the most exasperating as well as the most brilliant 'chaser in Europe. He had just returned from an unsuccessful attempt to prove himself the best horse in America when running only fourth in the Colonial Cup at Camden, South Carolina. "He ran great, though," says his trainer, Pat Taaffe, who as a jockey had scaled all the steeplechasing peaks even before he became Arkle's other half. "I wouldn't want to criticise Bobby Coonan," he adds in that accent as soft as the local water, "but we had seen on the film that all the winners came from behind, but then Christy jumps himself to the front, four out, and does one of his specials at the second last."

Captain Christy's "specials" have been the bane of punters' lives since he first exploded on to the 'chasing scene two seasons ago. He began by crashing Bobby Beasley out of the saddle within sight of home on consecutive English trips at Ascot and Haydock. Having soured up British supporters he then "Harvey Smithed" them by winning the 1974 Cheltenham Cup, and in four visits since has alternated between the abysmal, as in last season's two Cheltenham flops, and the superb, as when trouncing Pendil at Kempton last December, and when only just failing to give over two stone to April Seventh in the Whitbread.

His Irish fans suffered the same disasters, for his brilliant run in the Leopardstown Chase was counterbalanced by complete blow-outs in the Irish National and the Thyestes Chase. But Taaffe, 46, whose silvered hair is the only sign of the march of time, points out that it is not jumping that is Captain Christy's main trouble now. "It's just the very soft ground that he doesn't like, and he sulks in it. When he made all those mistakes he was only a novice. He is really a decent jumper now. Look how well he did in France last summer."

It is to France's varied obstacles that Captain Christy goes on Friday, his programme having an almost Solomon Grundy ring about it: "School on Saturday, run on Sunday, fly back Monday." Yet those who have criticised Taaffe's methods of coping with New Zealand owner Pat Samuel's global ambitions should remember how well they worked last June.

On his first run round the tight turns, not to mention the odd stone wall, at Enghein he won over 2½ miles, and followed that narrowly failing to last out the four miles of the Grand Steeplechase de Paris on the course at Auteuil. The £22,000 that he got for being second that day boosted his total winnings to over £76,822, and if he succeeds in only a third of his scheduled programme this season, he will become the first 'chaser to break the £100,000 barrier.

His English appointments are the King George VI Chase at Kempton, the Gold Cup, and very probably the Grand National if Uncle Cyril (Stein) can breathe some life into its bearded corpse. He might take the Irish National, which he won in 1974, as an alternative. Then, of course, there is the "Grand Steeple" in Paris, and Pat adds with simple pride: "We have already been invited back to America for next year's Colonial Cup."

Such aspirations all seem a long way from the peace of Pat Taaffe's hay barn. But a look at the condition of the compactly made champion (16.2 hands high, but more on flat racing than big rangy 'chaser lines) is reassuring. So too is the memory of his training sprint half an hour earlier up the side of a big thistle field full of cattle and sheep, and near a cottage where, I swear to you, there was a cow looking out of the front door.

The day before I'd seen his two great Irish rivals, Ten Up and Brown Lad, limbering up in Arkle's old haunts at Kilsallaghan, County Dublin. They will be running again before the end of the year. So too will Bula, who on Wednesday afternoon put Red Rum to shame at Haydock. The wraps are coming off the stars, and the clashes will be the highlights of the season. But the one they all have to beat is Captain Christy in his Dr Jekyll role.

In the end Captain Christy's legs betrayed him and he was never able to repeat those brilliant performances at Kempton and Cheltenham. Still he had his hour. So too did our next horse, albeit over much shorter distances. This was the pride of Scotland even if his name was Roman Warrior.

Lofty and the Warrior
September 21st 1975

Just occasionally, you get a race that simply makes you wonder at the power and glory and courage of the thoroughbred racehorse, the fastest weight-carrying creature the world has ever seen. It was like that when Roman Warrior won the Ayr Gold Cup for Scotland on Friday.

Of course, Roman Warrior is no stranger to making impressions since, at 17½ hands and well over half a ton, he is the biggest and heaviest Flat racehorse in the country, and his excellence over the last three seasons has long since established him as one of the fastest animals in training.

Yet Friday's performance against 22 opponents eclipsed all that had gone before. For, lumping a record ten stone in this most competitive of six-furlong handicaps, he was faced with unsuitably softened and patchy ground, and two of the biggest gambles seen this season. To turn the screw on the excitement it was the subject of these gambles, Lochnager and Import, who were his two greatest dangers as they reached for the line.

The dimensions of the triumph stretched on. For this Ayr Gold Cup was the richest sprint handicap in the country, and the biggest race of the year in Scotland, and in winning it for 31-year-old Nigel Angus's local stable, Roman Warrior was waving the largest banner yet for Scotland's prospects in the racing field.

It was an achievement strictly on cue, for there had been plenty of beating of the drum earlier during the immaculately run four days that make up the Western Meeting. On Wednesday, clerk of the course Bill McHarg had spoken out against the "south of Watford syndrome" that seeks to prune Scotland's six tracks as a "rationalisation" of racing's resources. "Let them put the axe elsewhere," he said. "We have the runners and the crowds coming to our courses, and with Scotland developing fast, this is not the time to cut down."

McHarg shares the duties at Ayr with Kit Patterson, and between the two of them they also run the other five Scottish courses at Perth, Hamilton, Edinburgh, Lanark and Kelso. And it was a native of Perth, businessman Pat Muldoon, who spoke out even more strongly at the Horse Race Writers' dinner on Thursday. "Racing in Scotland has never had an opportunity like this," he said. "For there is potential interest, and potential investment, on a vast scale. Soccer and racing have always been the two major sports for the Scotsman, and hooliganism on the terraces is now putting customers our way. And with the boom in North Sea oil and gas, there is at last a lot of money around for racing, if only there were some real salesmen to go out and hunt it."

Such tub-thumping seemed far away as I rode out with Nigel Angus's string in the hangover of Friday morning. Yet the seeds of progress were already there as I learnt that the most expensive yearling ever to come to Scotland (a £19,000 Manacle colt bought at Goffs' first magnificent sale in its new ultra-modern home) was due that afternoon, and up in front of the string was the greatest salesman of all, Roman Warrior. It is easy to say with hindsight, but if ever a horse looked fit to walk out into the spotlight, it was Roman Warrior that morning. "I don't think he has ever been so well," the stable's head lad and linch-pin, Charlie Williams, said.

However, in the best gentle-giant tradition, Roman Warrior forswears any aggressive use of his size. "He's a really kind horse, not colty in any way," said Hugh "Lofty" Brown from his distant perch in the sky. "Lofty," a 21-year-old from nearby Patna, towers over the other lads as Roman Warrior does over their horses. He has been the Warrior's devoted companion for over a year, just as he was to the stable's previous Ayr Gold Cup winner, Swinging Junior, in 1972.

"Lofty's" craggy features have not been notably improved by a little bit of local difficulty earlier this month. But it is of his love for his horse that the other lads speak in awe. "You know, he is always getting him eggs, and gallons of Guinness," they tell you. "And he wouldn't even leave Roman Warrior in the dope box to go and collect the champagne for the winning lad when he won here this summer."

After the cheers had finally settled on Friday afternoon, I saw Brown's devotion for myself. With the Angus stable only a quarter of a mile from the TV interview spot, it seemed a perfect opportunity to get "Lofty" up in front of the cameras to give a lad's eye view of a big winner. I sprinted down to find our hero just finishing the Warrior's post-race ablutions. He thought about the request for a moment, but then gave his shy gap-toothed smile and said: "No, thanks all the same. I think I will let my fella do all the talking."

Roman Warrior was a creature that has become all too rare in recent times—a truly charismatic flat race horse trained in the north. Over jumps there has been no such inferiority. Let's go back to the start of '76 and see a typical example of what the North does best. In this case doubly so.

Bargains Beat the System
January 1976

A big horse and a little horse walking round a windy North Yorkshire haybarn may be a long way from boring Old Father Time and that stork-carried baby, but last week they were the most hopeful symbols we could find for racing in 1976. For the careers of the tall, lanky hurdler, Night Nurse, and the short, whippety steeplechaser, Easby Abbey, and for that matter, of their 46-year-old trainer, Peter Easterby, are living answers to those gloom merchants who ask: "Will racing survive?"

The two horses are the biggest winners in their respective spheres this season, having won seven races worth over £30,000 between them. Yet early in their racing lives, you could have bought the pair of them for less than a family car. And their trainer, who now has more than sixty horses and a thousand acres under his care at Great Habton, near Malton, started 25 years ago with three horses, 25 acres, a share of £250 and no winners for three seasons. Ability to succeed runs in the family, for Easterby's brother Mick (who had the rest of the £250) started training eleven years later, fifteen miles closer to York, and with 65 winners totalling £67,000, not to mention his own 1,000-acre farm, was the leading Northern trainer on the Flat last season.

Yet for all these ritzy statistics, there is much more of the farmhouse clutter than the top racing-stable grandeur about Peter Easterby's establishment. It now boasts a new mile-and-a-quarter wood-shaving gallop, but the trainer freely admits that his original Vale of Pickering facilities were not too extensive. At one stage he was even reduced to surreptitiously galloping his horses in other men's cowfields when the herds were milking. Despite its present heroes and past winners like Champion Hurdler Saucy Kit, Royal Ascot success Godhill and Lincoln first Old Tom, it is a place where geese are treated strictly as geese right up until the royal swan-catcher begins to notice. The master puffs on his pipe in his twinkle-eyed way, and says: "This racing game's all right as long as you don't go expecting too much." What they expected from Easby Abbey when he started as a two-year-old seven summers ago was what the butcher would pay per pound, and since he was "a tiny narrow rabbit of a thing" that wasn't likely to buy too many bales of sawdust.

"He was useless on the Flat," said Easterby, as his fourteen-year-old son Timothy rode Easby Abbey proudly round the barn, "and absolutely crackers. No one could hold him. In the end we took him to Doncaster Sales, and he came back without even making three hundred pounds."

"So it came to pass," as the Christmas Lesson has it, that the "mad little rabbit" had one last chance, in a three-year-old hurdle at Market Rasen. The man to share this unenvied moment was none other than this season's Irish Sweeps hero, Paddy Broderick. "There were 24 runners who had never run before," he remembers. "And in the paddock the head lad took me on one side, and said: 'Now look, Brod, this thing jumps quick, but it's crazy. Miss the break or something, and watch after yourself.'"

Primed with these uninspiring instructions, Brod duly got himself a slow start, only to be carted past the whole field. Much more amazingly, he stayed there throughout. "After that, Easby Abbey won five straight," adds the jockey. "You would let him run away, and the others couldn't get to him."

The little horse (he is still only 15.2 hands) had found a metier, but it is still a long climb from getting home in a three-year-old summer scramble at Market Rasen, to winning thirteen races and running second in the Champion Hurdle. But even more unlikely peaks were to come. For, against the advice of his new partner, Ron Barry, Easby Abbey was put to the bigger obstacles, and after eight wins over two miles in the past two seasons, including the Benson and Hedges 'Chase last November, he won the Massey Ferguson at Cheltenham so easily over two-and-half miles last time out, that they are seriously considering three-quarters of a mile farther in the Gold Cup there next March.

Compared with that reformed delinquent, the story of the five-year-old Night Nurse has a silver-spoon ring to it, even though he showed nothing of the chunky good looks of his father, Falcon, but taking after the lanky plainness of his mother, Florence Nightingale. (Before you titter, she was cleverly named, being by Above Suspicion out of Panacea.)

He made only 1,300 guineas at the Newmarket Yearling Sales, and unsurprisingly Night Nurse was too immature to win in six attempts on the Flat as a two-year-old. But even though he won at Ripon in 1974, it was over hurdles that his weak-looking hocks really revealed their power. He won five out of seven last season, and his four wins this time culminated in the Irish Sweeps. It all draws the bold Broderick into saying: "This is the best jumper I have ever sat on."

Forgetting all the oft-repeated problems that best top-class Flat racing, a visit to Yorkshire shows that National Hunt racing will survive because of the circumstances that can throw up a trail-blazing pair like Easby Abbey and Night Nurse.

Looking at little Easby, who has the deep indentation of a sinus operation below his left eye as the only scar from an already long and honourable career, I thought back to Dublin at Christmas. Two horsemen were arguing about the price of a horse in the usual "telephone numbers". In justification of his argument one leant back in his chair and said: "Look, you are not just buying your owner a horse—you are giving him a dream."

But the dream is not confined to the small owner and the scratch-bred horse. Lord Howard de Walden is one of the wealthiest men in the land, Lanzarote one of his own equine blue bloods. The horse brought him great success but in March 1976 there was the dream of Lanzarote becoming the first horse to double up his previous hurdling championship with victory in steeplechasing's top race, The Cheltenham Gold Cup. Some of us thought it all too easy and so there is a sadly fatal optimism in this piece written just four days before Lanzarote's death at Cheltenham.

Too Prophetic for Comfort
March 1977

When (not if) Lanzarote's sweaty, white-starred face looks out from the tumult of the Cheltenham winner's enclosure on Thursday it will be easy to forget that along the way he has had enough problems to daunt even the toughest camel on the pumice stone island from which he got his name.

Lanzarote will be hot favourite to take the steeplechasing crown in the £30,000 Piper Champagne Gold Cup, and his connections read like a roll-call of a racing Debrett—owned and bred by the present Senior Steward, Lord Howard de Walden, trained by the legendary Fred Winter and ridden by the reigning champion jockey, John Francome. Yet however flawless the victory may be, none of these paragons would ever describe what has led up to it as "easy".

For a start, he will be the first Champion Hurdler to graduate to steeplechasing triumph in the Gold Cup's 53-year history. And even when he was winning the hurdle title in that epic race with Comedy of Errors in 1974, he was renowned for a casualness over the obstacles that would have been fatal over the bigger fences.

"To be honest, I was against him going 'chasing," said Lord Howard with engaging candour last week. "I felt it would be terrible if he made one of his bloomers, and broke his bloody neck at Taunton!" This attitude kept the horse over hurdles last year, but all along Fred Winter remembered how well Lanzarote had jumped when, in an attempt to make him treat hurdles better, he had been schooled over fences two-and-a-half years ago.

"The thing was that he was so sensible," says Fred. "Then he went to America and handled their different-looking fences very well, and so we had to start over here, and even though everyone must remember that he is a novice, he has won all his three races with aplomb."

Winter won two Gold Cups as a jockey, but although he has been champion trainer five times, this blue riband has continued to elude him. His nearest miss

Lanzarote and his trainer Fred Winter in March 1977. His Gold Cup attempt was to end in tragedy (Gerry Cranham)

was in 1973, when Pendil was beaten by a short head, and two years ago Soothsayer and Bula were second and third to Ten Up. John Francome is confident that they can lay the bogy this year, although he too has some vivid reservations.

"Lanzarote is the best horse I have ridden," he says. "He doesn't pull, you can put him anywhere in a race, but at the fences you have got to organise him. If you want him to stand off, you have to make sure he comes up, and if he needs to shorten you have got to get hold of him properly. He still keeps his back pretty flat, like a hurdler, but he keeps his arse good and low like Bula used to so even if he does belt one I think he should be all right." Lanzarote punters, disturbed by the complexities of all that, may like to remember that Winter has described Francome as "the best jockey to present a horse at fence that I have ever seen."

But the transition from hurdles to fences has been the least, if hopefully the last, of Lanzarote's troubles. Our witness is the horse's sixty-year-old lad, Harry Foster, as he rode him over Lambourn Downs on Wednesday. "He may be a nine-year-old," said Harry, giving the gleaming black rump behind him a hefty slap, "but I honestly tell you that he is better now than he has ever been. I wish he was in the Champion Hurdle too, then I *would* have a bet. He has had so much trouble with his corns, his back, his skin that it's only this season that he has been a hundred per cent."

Lanzarote looked suitably unimpressed with all this praise as we mooched home down the lane, but Harry's verdict was echoed by Lanzarote's old partner, Richard Pitman. "I have never seen him look so well," he said. "I think it has been the guv'nor's greatest training performance. Those corns (which used to come up in his near forefoot just like a human's) were such a puzzle. I remember that he went lame with them on the morning he was flying to Ireland, but he travelled just the same, and after he had run all right the guv'nor said: 'Okay, he's a man now—we can't molly-coddle him any more.' "

Such last-minute panics were recalled by Lord Howard de Walden: "Of course, Fred always eats cigarettes before a big race, but I remember that when Lanzarote won the Champion Hurdle his feet were so dodgy that Fred made him walk round the paddock on the grass rather than the tarmac."

Yet the corns, for which Winter still equips him with a "three-quarters" shoe, were a problem that arrived after Lanzarote had begun to show championship potential, winning a sequence of races culminating in the Imperial Cup with 12st 5lb on his back. The real wonder to everyone who remembers his early days is that he showed any ability at all.

Lanzarote started his career as a two-year-old with the experienced Jack Waugh at Newmarket, who after three runs—the last in blinkers "to see if they would liven him up"—reported him "very, very slow". Next year he moved to Ernie Weymes at Middleham, who in eight attempts won a modest fifteen-furlong race with him at Edinburgh. That was enough for Weymes to dissuade Lord Howard from selling Lanzarote. He says now: "I remember he got knocked all over the place at Edinburgh and still won, and I thought there must be something about him after all. But I never thought he would make a hurdler. He was so big and weak he would stumble over a matchstick."

However, Lanzarote did adapt, winning the second of his two hurdle races in that first season. His rider then, Paul Kelleway, remembers, "A big shell of a horse with the right idea, but very weak." The jumping world is littered with horses like this, very few of whom ever develop. For them to do so, something more than the skill and patience of the Winter team is needed.

It is a quality referred to by everyone who has had anything to do with Lanzarote, from Lord Howard in his regal London office to Jim Fitzgerald in the green fields of County Kildare, where Lanzarote was foaled just nine years ago next month. It is something that has made delving into his past a labour of love—a deep, shining honesty about everything he does. Many equine champions, like their human counterparts, have their prima donna side. But Lanzarote is a Henry Cooper of a horse, a powerful tiger on the course, yet gentle and quiet off it.

"When he came to us," says Fred Winter, crinkling those tough but understanding eyes, "he looked like a herring. But he always had that charm, he wanted to do his best." Even if Lanzarote fails on Thursday he has long since shown that with his attitude even a camel may conquer.

Lanzarote's death was mourned by a much wider circle than his own stable. Indeed it is one of the characteristics of a great horse that they can inspire interest and affection from far and wide. One such was the 1978 and '79 Champion Hurdler, Monksfield. He even had a book written about him before he tried for the treble in 1980. It was as good an excuse as any for a trip across the water.

Monksfield—A Prophet and his Star
March 2nd 1980

The biggest star in the hurdling game stayed at home on Thursday, but the prophet made the long journey from Moynalty to Wexford, and for a change was not without honour in his own country. The star is Monskfield, the little bay horse with the huge heart and the swinging left leg, who bids to win his third consecutive Champion Hurdle at Cheltenham in ten days' time. The prophet is Monksfield's young trainer, Dessie McDonagh, who, through a long winter of doubt and criticism, has kept a belief in his horse which looks like being justified. Last Saturday, Monskfield ran a magnificent race at Leopardstown to re-establish himself as hot favourite to retain the crown.

It was mild down at Wexford races on Thursday. The sun has been out in Ireland these past few days, and Monksfield, with his summer coat almost

Champion hurdler Monksfield and his trainer Dessie McDonagh step out on an icy February morning in 1980 (Chris Smith)

through on his magnificently muscled eight-year-old frame, has reacted with relish. Dessie McDonogh, too, has been walking on air, but when you consider what he and his horse have been through, you can perhaps forgive a certain dryness in the smile that comes easily to the heavy-lidded eyes in that quick fox's face.

For although, at 34, Limerick-born Dessie has accomplished more in his seven years as a trainer than most people could dream about, he remains something of an outsider to the main Irish racing family. "A man," as one stalwart told me on Thursday, "not totally at peace with his life." He has made Monskfield into the most popular Irish horse since Arkle, and also last year proved he was no one-horse wonder by saddling Stranfield to win the coveted Supreme Novice Hurdle two races before Monksfield's triumph at Cheltenham. But he is still unsupported by the big-league owners, and his 26-strong stable, twenty miles south of the border in Moynalty, Co Meath, has not had a winner since last July.

His two runners on Thursday did not change the pattern, but their turn-out, and their efforts (one was fifth and the other third at 16–1) confirmed that there was nothing wrong with McDonogh's ability, however unorthodox his methods may sometimes be. "I have never doubted myself for one moment," he confided, "but this winter has been difficult, with everybody telling me that 'Monkey' was gone, and we should retire him."

The problems reached crisis point when Monksfield, after three already unsuccessful runs, trailed in last one watery day at Navan last December. "It was a terrible moment," said Dessie on Thursday, "and we took some terrible flak. But I was sure the horse was wrong in himself. We took his pulse and it was 126, and even after half an hour it was still 108—much too high."

The general view had been that Monksfield, an eight-year-old entire horse, had lost his racing enthusiasm to thoughts of the stallion's life his labours had assured him. Ironically, events were to prove that it was indeed Monksfield's sexual status, unique amongst top-class racers of his age, that was the problem. During the cold weather, his body produced too many hormones, making his blood too thick. "Like the engine oil in a car," is McDonogh's graphic description. With treatment involving more fluid intake and folic acid tablets, and above all with the onset of warmer weather, the imbalance righted itself and the improvement soon became apparent to McDonogh.

It was not the first time that the end of a racing career had seemed imminent. Two years ago Monksfield got an infection in the hock, and his condition fell away so sharply that a local "witch doctor" was called in before veterinary science found a cure.

Throughout that crisis, and the more recent one, McDonogh has tended his horse with the fierce possessiveness you can understand from a man who both bought Monksfield for a derisory 720 guineas and built his box when encased in plaster.

All that and much, much more is lovingly and entertainingly chronicled in Jonathan Powell's biography of Monksfield, just published. While declaring the interest of having written the foreword, I must still recommend the book as required reading for anyone who likes the true colour and smell of racing, and who has some interest in one of sport's most remarkable romances.

"Time is going to hang terrible heavy until Cheltenham," said McDonogh on Thursday, as he thought of the pressures ahead. Hoping for history to repeat itself for a second time may be tempting providence, but study the story and this prophet and his star, and you would not bet against it.

Although Monksfield could only finish fourth at Cheltenham that year and retired to stud at the end of the season, his story is a classic of the little outfit taking on the big batallions. In flat racing, with its more expensive investment, such a case is much, much rarer. That was why the saga of Soba, the original bargain basement filly, caught everyone's imagination. She was well worth the visit.

Local Lass Makes Good
September 5th 1982

She may be female, four-legged and not exactly fantastic at cricket, but Soba is what the summer has been missing. The genuine all-Yorkshire sporting hero.

A year ago, this plain-headed chestnut filly was just one of racing's forgotten army. A locally-bred, family-trained, unglamorously-ridden little two-year-old whose best effort in nine attempts was to finish third under bottom weight in a modest race at Musselburgh. This season, trainer David Chapman and his same unsung, unseeking team have now sent Soba out from their weathered red-brick Yorkshire farmhouse near Stillington to win nine of her eleven races, and when she took the most recent, the Great St Wilfrid Handicap at Ripon, the cheers were almost loud enough to bring that bishop back to his seventh-century birthplace.

The improvement (over four stones in the official handicap ratings) is unmatched in present times, and besides the endearing homespun qualities, it is centred around that most exciting of all horse-racing elements, brilliant searing early speed. Almost half a ton of muscled-up athlete caged in the starting stalls, and then suddenly catapulted forward to reach over forty mph in less than forty yards.

"The moment you gather the reins up," says Wetherby jockey David Nicholls, himself so unfamous that his future seemed to be in racing in Cyprus, "Soba dives at the front of the stalls. If the starter hasn't pressed his button she can be rocking back when the gates open. But if we time it right, the race is over."

Between 8 May and 25 June, Soba won all her six races. Yet, according to Nicholls, it was only in the last, the Gosforth Park Cup at Newcastle, that Soba "really hit the traps". Even sceptical southerners had now begun to take notice, but when the filly got beaten and injured her back next time up at Ayr, it was generally considered that the run was over. This was still the mood when, only seventeen days later, Soba travelled 300 miles south for the Stewards' Cup at Goodwood, drew the least-favoured number one starting position, and then gave a rodeo-bucking display on the way to the stalls. But supercilious sympathy turned to standing ovation as the blinkered filly spreadeagled the most important sprint handicap of the year, and wrote the most romantic racing chapter since Red Rum gave up jumping Becher's Brook for a new career opening betting shops.

Being a tough Yorkshire lass—the nuptials between her mother, Mild Wind, and father, Most Secret, took place at Easthorpe Stud near Castle Howard, and cost a mere £350—Soba has not been preening herself in the box during the month since Goodwood. She has run three more times, the only defeat coming in a photo-finish at Newcastle ("I could have won but hadn't the heart to hit her," says Nicholls), and she now tilts at even bigger things. The Scarbrough Stakes on Wednesday is to be followed by the Diadem Stakes at Ascot and, all being well, by the final great European sprint of the year, the Prix de l'Abbaye at Long-champ on Arc de Triomphe Day.

Those places have the smack of the jet-set and the world stage about them, a charge that no one could level at Mowbray House, a rather grandiloquent title for the homely two-hundred-acre farm where for the past thirty years David and Marion Chapman have grown barley, raised children and, in more recent times, performed psychiatric miracles on a whole series of equine rogues and sinners. Indeed, David Nicholls only forsook the steamy delights of Nicosia racecourse last spring for the prospect of renewed success on Higham Grey, another Chapman inmate who had previously acquired an unenviable reputation for downing tools in mid-contest.

Compared with Higham Grey and company, Soba is almost the queen of the crop. She is owned, and was bred, thirty miles away in Boston Spa by Chapman's sister, Muriel Hills, who was so impressed by the foal's decorum that she wanted to call it Sobersides. That's a name that still looked fitting as the White Rose wonder horse stood out in the sunshine last week.

Suddenly you get to the moment when you ask the magician about his trick. What is the secret of Soba? In a multi-million-pound business where all round the world canny brains are scheming the best way to speed and sharpen the thoroughbred racehorse, what is the system of the quiet Yorkshireman who himself always drives the horsebox to the races and to gallops at Wetherby Park? How does he exercise the champion?

Chapman shifts his feet, looks to his wife and to Soba's friend and stable-girl, Linda Macauley, for help, and then says simply: "Well, I don't believe in riding them out. Soba's mother broke her hip after getting loose on the road. I take them off to work when I think they need it. On the other days, I just turn them out here, in the field. I think that's best, it relaxes them."

Throw away your books, you theorists. Put down your cheque-books, you pundits. Come and watch Soba do it for Yorkshire on Wednesday. After all, you'll be seeing it Nature's way.

Incredibly that was only the half-way stage for Soba. For after winning the next week at Doncaster and running well at Ascot she retired for the winter and then in 1983 proved herself in the highest class of all. Winner of the Group 2 King George Stakes at Goodwood, she was also four times second to Habibti, the horse of the year, including being beaten by only a length in Longchamp's Prix de L'Abbaye, Europe's sprint of the season. Soba, the humble-bred Yorkshire lass, then went to stud and was certified in foal to the brilliant, expensive and unhappy-fated Golden Fleece before that horse's untimely death in April '84.

The death of any horse is always a sadness. But it's never worse than when they are snuffed out in the heat of the race itself.

Ekbalco R.I.P.
November 13th 1983

Tragedy came brutally out of the cupboard at Newcastle yesterday. Ekbalco, the best horse in the North, smashed his shoulder when he fell and had to be shot just as he was challenging for the lead in the Fighting Fifth Hurdle.

That fall, at the second last, left the champion, Gaye Brief, to stroll home from his pacemaker, Migrator. But long before the winning post had been reached, most of us had our binoculars switched to where the last sad rites of the Ekbalco disaster were being enacted.

In every way this was the bitter side of National Hunt racing. At one moment Ekbalco—winner of ten races and over £50,000—was cruising up to the lead, half a ton of magnificent bay power and muscle, the very symbol of the galloping horse in motion. At the next he had taken off too soon, and crashed so heavily into the ground that his shoulder was a distorted mass of broken bones.

Suddenly Jonjo O'Neill was no longer a jockey, but a nursemaid to the dying. The man who only on Friday clocked up the fastest fifty winners in a jumping season was ignoring his own problems as he called across to the vet to come over and put Ekbalco out of his agony.

When a horse who has given so much pleasure, and drawn so much attention, is dealt so unceremonious a dispatch, we have to ask about the brutality of the business. But the facts are that Ekbalco's injuries were such that nothing short of a veterinary miracle could mend them, and even that would involve long days and months of unexplainable, scarcely endurable, suffering. It's no fun to write these words, but in a case like this it is best to speed the friendly bullet. Quite simply, it's the kindest thing to do.

Anyone who still feels that racing people are into animal abuse should talk to jockeys who have had an experience like yesterday's. Five times I've been through the moment of having a horse who was my ally crumple up as the vet puts a shot through his skull. It's all too easy to remember each choking time, and simple to understand why O'Neill was streaming tears as he ran back to the weighing-room. It was true that his choice of Ekbalco yesterday cost him the ride on the Mackeson Gold Cup winner, Pounentes, at Cheltenham, but as the champion elect came in, what hurt was that he had lost a friend.

Yet to sign off a sad day for racing, we should record whom Ekbalco's death upset most. Jenny Moffatt, the wife of the horse's assistant trainer, used to ride him out every morning. In the way of the racing circus, her stable duties also involved leading up the unraced Humyak House in the last race. Jenny did her job before a race in which Jonjo rode his 51st winner. But she couldn't stop the tears falling. She won't forget yesterday too quickly.

That was the worst that can happen. Let's sign off with the best. And it's interesting to see straightaway how near to each other those two extremes keep on the racecourse as well as off it. That only reinforces the thought that, great frivolity though racing may be, it still has truths that stand the test of time.

The Leap Into Immortality
March 18th 1984

For fully five minutes Burrough Hill Lad lay motionless by the last jump, his jockey trapped beneath him. The men with the green tarpaulin got ready as the vet hurried over to perform the last rites. No, this is not one of Jenny Pitman's famous dreams. It is exactly what happened four years ago.

Somehow you need that memory to put into perspective all the euphoric scenes in the Cheltenham winners' enclosure to appreciate just how long, hard and downright dangerous had been the road travelled by our new Gold Cup winner before the admirable Phil Tuck rode him back in sweaty triumph on Thursday.

In the last two months Burrough Hill Lad and his gifted lady trainer have built up such public momentum that last week's result seemed almost inevitable. But without taking away an oat from the shrewd, sympathetic and supremely confident manner in which Jenny Pitman has brought "Buzby" (his stable name) to the present peak, it is Burrough Hill Lad's achievement in overcoming such things as that 1980 disaster at Kempton which truly show the mountains that a National Hunt champion has to climb.

On 18 January 1980 Burrough Hill Lad was still three months short of his fourth birthday, a huge, raw, dark-brown baby trained then by that great wheelchair survivor, the former jockey Jimmy Harris. "He was a big, black, spotty thing when he first came to us," said Jimmy on Friday. "But once he got himself organised you could see that he had real potential, and he had already won twice before he got into trouble at Kempton."

The accident which grabbed "Buzby" is one that stalks every horse that thunders over a hurdle—the casual stride, the loss of balance, and then half a ton of horseflesh landing on three foot of neck at upwards of 33 miles an hour. "I thought we were going to lose him," remembers Harris, "and even when he did get up all he wanted to do was to lie down again. And when we got him home he was so crippled that he couldn't bend his neck to drink."

Courage at the bottom of the well is one essential quality, but to pull through his assorted dramas Burrough Hill Lad has surely needed a guardian angel too. Who is to say that the great binoculars in the sky weren't looking down when Phil Tuck's left rein broke at Warwick earlier in that always hazardous first season? Or when the now sadly injured Jon Haynes flew off him when in front at the final flight in his following race? When leg trouble threatened the horse's career on three subsequent occasions? Or, finally, when his early chasing days included a tendency to ignore about one fence in seven? "He never actually fell on a racecourse," said his then jockey Colin Brown. "But he put me into orbit at Haydock and Cheltenham and he got buried out schooling one morning."

After the Kempton crash the angel took the leathery and unmistakably tangible form of Ronnie Longford, the horse osteopath who for countless years has almost been doing an equine version of "take up your bed and walk". Jimmy Harris still can't believe it. "After ten days Burrough Hill Lad was that bad that we had to lift him into the van to take him to Ronnie Longford's clinic at Banbury. Ronnie pushed and prodded at his back and neck, said his head was on wrong and vertebrae were out of place, and by the time we got home the horse was bucking and kicking."

Through all these excitements only one of the actors has always remained on stage—the owner Stan Riley, the farmer and small businessman from Burrough Hill in Leicestershire who nine years ago shelled out £450 for his unsuccessful mare Green Monkey to receive the favours of the local stallion Richboy. "I didn't know whether they would produce something for the flat or the jumps," said Stan on Friday. "But when we saw how big he was it was obvious that jumping would be his game, though he galloped so well around the fields at home that I was sure he would be something."

Today that prophecy has been fulfilled to the tune of thirteen wins from thirty races in five seasons, and £110,939 in prize money. Even if these handsome

Happiness is a dream come true. Jenny Pitman holds Burrough Hill Lad after his Gold Cup triumph at Cheltenham in 1984 (Chris Smith)

187

pickings are less than half what some as yet unsung three-year-old-old will earn for his sixth (and last?) appearance, in the Derby at Epsom this June, Stan Riley's involvement would match any owner's. (That is excepting the Champion hurdler Dawn Run's galloping granny Charmian Hill, who was tossed high in the air by her supporters on Tuesday, a precedent mercifully not attempted by fans of the rather heavier-engined Jenny Pitman on Thursday.)

In pursuit of his perfection, and to nail the lie that good chasers come only with shamrock in their ears, Stan Riley has exerted his owner's prerogative to change Burrough Hill Lad's training quarters twice. There's no doubt that he has found the right home with Mrs Pitman.

But there's also no doubting Riley's feelings when he remembers the bad days. "When Burrough Hill Lad lay there at Kempton, I felt sure he was finished," says the owner. "And I thought back to the South Notts point-to-point on Easter Monday in 1949, the first race of my first horse Simon VI. He finished fourth of sixteen, and dropped dead walking back."

Such caveats recall the other side of Cheltenham, and most of all Childown, whose leg snapped on Thursday and who had to wait for the vet's dispatch, his head cradled in the beleaguered Francome's arms. In human terms the losses are rarely as tragic, and amongst the beaten army—some drunken, some despondent and, sadly, one celebrated but ungracious loser—it was worth hearing Jimmy Harris's words from the wheelchair about the horse he set on the road to stardom. "I have no regrets," said Harris. "I am proud to have had a Gold Cup winner in the stable. I think we all played our part."

A man in a wheelchair still at peace with the game which broke him, and praising a horse he lost. It's the sort of moment when you can forgive the wretched business almost anything.

Mind you, the same can't always be said about the readers. Not too long ago I was being quizzed by some TV punter as to how I spent the off-screen hours. Your correspondent immediately launched into a long dissertation about the creative pains of composing the weekly Sunday Times *piece. My self-justifying harangue might have crept into the second hour if the unfortunate questioner had not stopped things short: "Oh yes. I've seen the by-line but I didn't think you actually wrote that stuff . . ."*

What could he mean?

Index